Bloom's

GUIDES

Homer's
The Odyssey

CURRENTLY AVAILABLE

The Adventures of Huckleberry Finn
All the Pretty Horses
Animal Farm
Beloved
Brave New World
The Catcher in the Rye
The Chosen
The Crucible
Cry, the Beloved Country
Death of a Salesman
Fahrenheit 451
The Glass Menagerie
The Grapes of Wrath
Great Expectations
The Great Gatsby
Hamlet
The Handmaid's Tale
The House on Mango Street
I Know Why the Caged Bird Sings
The Iliad
Lord of the Flies
Macbeth
Maggie: A Girl of the Streets
The Member of the Wedding
The Metamorphosis
Of Mice and Men
1984
The Odyssey
One Hundred Years of Solitude
Pride and Prejudice
Ragtime
Romeo and Juliet
Slaughterhouse-Five
The Scarlet Letter
Snow Falling on Cedars
A Streetcar Named Desire
A Tale of Two Cities
The Things They Carried
To Kill a Mockingbird

Bloom's
GUIDES

Homer's
The Odyssey

Edited & with an Introduction
by Harold Bloom

CHELSEA HOUSE
PUBLISHERS
An imprint of Infobase Publishing

Bloom's Guides: The Odyssey

Copyright ©2007 by Infobase Publishing
Introduction ©2007 by Harold Bloom

Chelsea House
An imprint of Infobase Publishing
132 West 31st Street
New York NY 10001

ISBN-10: 0-7910-9299-2
ISBN-13: 978-0-7910-9299-6

Library of Congress Cataloging-in-Publication Data
Homer's The Odyssey / [edited by] Harold Bloom.
    p. cm. — (Bloom's guides)
Includes bibliographical references and index.
ISBN 0-7910-9299-2 (hardcover)
1. Homer. Odyssey. 2. Greek literature—History and criticism. I. Bloom, Harold. II. Title. III. Series.
    PA4167.H66 2007
    883'.01—dc22   2006031093

Contributing Editor: Thomas Schmidt
Cover design by Takeshi Takahashi
Printed in the United States of America
Bang EJB 10 9 8 7 6 5 4 3 2 1
This book is printed on acid-free paper.

All links and web addresses were checked and verified to be correct at the time of publication. Because of the dynamic nature of the web, some addresses and links may have changed since publication and may no longer be valid.

Contents

Introduction

HAROLD BLOOM

Though an epic, the *Odyssey* has many attributes of the literary genre called the "romance," a marvelous story more inclined to fantasy than to realistic representation. Homer turns in the *Odyssey* to what might be defined as realistic descriptions of the marvelous, a formula apt for the hero Odysseus, who must avoid disasters as varied as being devoured by a one-eyed monster or drowning in freezing waters. The great burden for Odysseus is that his implacable enemy is Poseidon the sea god, and yet Odysseus is an island king who can get back to Ithaca only by passing through the realm of Poseidon. This immense difficulty can be surmounted only by a quester of endless resource: cunning, courageous, stubborn above all. The very name "Odysseus" (which became "Ulysses" in Latin) means either a curse's victim or an avenger who carries a curse to others. This ambiguity hints both at the sufferings of Odysseus and at his dangerousness to his enemies. He is a survivor: prudent, wise, perhaps a little cold. You do not want to be in one boat with him, however admirable you judge him to be: you may well drown, but he will reach land.

It has been argued that the *Odyssey*, for all its wonders, founds its storytelling upon the exclusion of surprise. That seems to be one of the prime aesthetic virtues of the poem: it insists upon working though its own suppositions, and so plays fair with the reader. Aristotle praises Homer for centering both the epics upon a single action, which in the *Odyssey* is the voyage home to Ithaca. The rugged simplicity of Homer's tale is its principal power; the story gives us a hero so skilled and tactful that he rarely abandons the long view. And yet the Odysseus who at last returns to his wife, son, and kingdom, is more than just two decades older and wiser than when he left; he is indeed a hero who has weathered archaic and magical adventures that are somehow at variance with his ultimate quest for simplicity. Odysseus has reemerged from a world that we identify as dreams and nightmares, and his embrace of an ordinary reality has in it a reputation of fantasy as such. The hero has refused victimization by gods and by demons, and his triumph heartens the reader, who beholds in Odysseus an emblem of our heroic longing for the commonplace. Homer does not seem to reflect upon the irony that his hero finally refuses all enchantments even though the hero's very name indicates that Odysseus himself is an enchanter, a troublemaker for nearly everyone whom he ever encounters.

Many critics have seen Odysseus as the one figure in all literature who most uniquely establishes and sustains his own identity. Certainly, few characters in Western literature have so firm a conviction as to precisely how their identity is to be confirmed and renewed. Despite the wisdom of Odysseus, his identity is not easily maintained, since his great enemy is the ultimate shapeshifter, the god of all ocean. Athena, the hero's champion and guide, is well aware of the odds against Odysseus, and the hero himself knows how much he needs her assistance if he is to survive. His longing for return seems already an allegory for the soul's yearning, in Platonism and beyond, though Homer certainly did not see his Odysseus as a religious pilgrim. Ithaca, in the poem, means something realistic and simple, and yet going home, against the sea god's opposition, is bound to suggest transcendental elements as well.

Odysseus matures throughout the poem; he never suffers without learning from the experience, and his appeal to Athena may well be that he becomes more and more like her, except that he does not want to attain the detachment of the goddess, despite his own tendency to coldness and cunning when they seem essential for survival.

James Joyce thought that Odysseus was the one "complete" hero in literature and therefore chose Homer's voyager as the model for Leopold Bloom in *Ulysses.* Compared to Joyce's Bloom, who is a paradigm of kindness and sweetness, Homer's Odysseus is capable of great savagery, but this is never savagery for its own sake, nor will Odysseus resort to force until guile has failed him. The hero's comprehensiveness induces him to be pragmatic and to be concerned primarily with the question, will it work? Americans therefore are likely to find something very American in Odysseus, even though our writers have yet to give us a convincing version of Homer's hero. The closest of all our literary characters to one aspect of Odysseus is Mark Twain's Huck Finn, whose innocent cunning sometimes suggests a childlike transformation of the Homeric hero into an American survivor. Perhaps all of American history is a closer analogue to the *Odyssey*: the American dream finally involves a hope of returning home, wiser and richer than when we departed from there in order to experience warfare, marvelous enchantments, and the forging of a self-reliant identity strong enough to bring us back to where we began.

Biographical Sketch

Almost nothing is known about Homer's life. Chance and the laborious scribes of Byzantium have preserved for us 30,000 lines of hexameter poetry in the form of two long epic poems which reach back into the dim past of a nascent Greece. The classical Greeks referred to the author of this text as "Homer," whom they usually referred to as simply "the poet." But aside from the fact that this text exists, and that Homer is a man's name, there are no sure evidences of his life. An ancient tradition holds that he was a blind bard from Chios, but at one point or another seven different Greek *poleis* were vying for the honor of being his birthplace, so such claims must be met with circumspection. His place of birth, the era in which he lived, the circumstances of his life, his methods of composition, even his very existence, are questions which will never decisively be answered.

Both the *Iliad* and the *Odyssey* begin with invocations of the Muse. Homer would have said that the Muse was a goddess, daughter of Mnemosyne (memory), who possessed and inspired him to become her mouthpiece and sing. A modern reader would probably take it as a metaphor: but just who, or what, is Homer's muse? A goddess? A trope for the divine faculty in man, the imagination of a solitary, creative poet? Or a formulaic system of oral poetry, the patrimony of a long tradition of bards?

From the rediscovery of Homer in Western Europe in the fourteenth century until roughly the end of the eighteenth century, it was taken for granted that Homer composed with the aid of writing. "Homer," writes Pope, "is universally allow'd to have had the greatest Invention of any Writer whatever." The moment usually chosen as the inauguration of the so-called Homeric Question, which plunged this whole picture into doubt, is the publication of a pamphlet by F. A. Wolf in 1795 called *Prolegomena ad Homerum*. In it, Wolf claimed that Homer was pre-literate, and so the texts that have come down to us could not possibly have been penned by

Homer himself. He proposed that "Homer" had been a great oral bard of the past, the fragments of whose poetry were transmitted orally until they were compiled during the time of Peisistratus in Athens.

While Wolf's hypothesis of a later Athenian compilation is no longer credible, his more fundamental premise—that Homer was pre-literate and his epics not the creation of one mind—was groundbreaking and quickly won adherents. Homerists quickly found themselves divided into two opposing camps: the Analysts, who laboriously and untiringly deconstructed the Homeric epics, trying to penetrate to those ancient nuggets buried within, which were from the authentic Homer, still alive but barely visible through murk of later editors, compilers, and imposters; and the Unitarians, who argued for the essential unity and integrity of the Homeric poems as the product of one man.

Philologists quarreled, and progress on the Homeric Question stagnated. Then, a brilliant study by a young scholar recast the entire question. Classicists and the common reader alike had observed formulaic elements of Homer's poetry, in his epithets and repetitions, but is was Milman Parry, in a French dissertation in 1928, who first cogently described their necessity to an oral bard and their scope and importance to Homeric diction. The Homeric poems are composed in a complex and exacting meter called dactylic hexameter. Greek meter is based upon vowel length, and not upon stress, as English meter is. A hexameter line is composed of six "feet," and a foot is either a long syllable followed by two shorts (a dactyl) or two long syllables (a spondee). The first five "feet" of a line can be dactyls or spondees, but the final foot must have two syllables, either long-long (a spondee) or long-short (a trochee). To complicate things further, word breaks can only fall in prescribed places in a line. Any beginning Greek student who tries his pen at a few lines of hexameter will immediately be awed that Homer left us 30,000.

Given the complexity of this meter, Parry proposed that the *raison d'etre* of the Homeric formula was the pressure of extemporaneous composition of poetry in dactylic hexameter.

The difficulty of improvising in meter necessitated certain formulary expressions to aid in that composition. "[Homer's] diction, in so far as it is made up of formulae, is entirely due to the influence of meter.... Formulary diction ... was created by the desire of bards to have ready at hand words and expressions which could easily be put into heroic verse."[1] By a comparative study of Homer with another tradition of oral poetry that is still alive in Yugoslavia, Parry showed that oral bards never just recite from rote memorization; rather, they improvise, and each recitation creates a new poem. Their language is equipped with various ready-made phrases that fill metrical slots and aid in each re-creation.

The essential point, and, according to Parry, the proof that Homer is in a tradition of oral poetry, is that the formulary system is of great "economy" and "extension." The system is economical because there is only a single formulaic expression for each fundamental idea in a given metrical environment. In other words, though there are six different epithets commonly applied to Odysseus, each is metrically unique. Parry's notion of "extension" refers simply to the variety of metrical forms available. The troubling implication of this is that the system and meter choose the words for you, not vaguer considerations like context or pathos. The meter itself creates the poetry.

Lest this become too abstract, take the first line of Book IX as an example. King Alcinous has asked Odysseus to reveal his name, and tell his story to the hall of banqueters. The first line of the book begins, *"ton d' apameibomenos prosephe..."*, ("and then he spoke to him in reply ..."). Homer now has the two final feet of the line to name the speaker, and the only form of "Odysseus" that fits in that slot is *polymetis Odysseus* (Odysseus of many wiles). So the meter necessitates that Odysseus become *polymetis* at that moment.

From his investigation of noun-epithet formulae, Parry posited that style of Homer *in toto* is formulary. The poet did not have his freedom to choose his diction, and so much in the poems is not intentionally meaningful. Such memorable epithets as "rose-fingered dawn," for example, would not carry semantic weight, but would be a mere verse filler, a wrapping to fit the idea into a verse. Parry exhorted us to create a new "aesthetics of traditional style."

Based on Parry's extrapolations, old-fashioned criticism of Homer was deemed irrelevant. Ruskin had written about the pathos of a dead corpse interred in the "life-giving earth," but this pathos, according to the fiercest Parryists, was alien to Homer. Albert Lord, a disciple of Parry, called this kind of reading a new "'pathetic fallacy,' in that it attributes to an innocent epithet a pathos felt only by the critic, but not acknowledged or perhaps even dreamed of by the poet."

The Parry-Lord hypothesis was the dominant paradigm in Homeric studies for many years, but it has had the natural life-cycle of any radical idea: a brood of disciples followed by sober reappraisal. He was the product of a particular intellectual moment, usually called structuralism, which sought to uncover simple principles and correspondences beneath superficial diversity. The current attitude in Homeric criticism is that Parry's findings—though immensely important—do not support this grandiose restructuring of Homeric aesthetics. His great insight was to link the formulaic element in Homer to an oral tradition, but he overemphasized how constrictive the formulaic element was on Homer.

Consider the following statistics about the use of the name Odysseus in the nominative case in the *Odyssey*. It occurs with an epithet 159 times, and without and epithet 158 times. That alone should give us pause: How demanding can this system of epithets be if it only accounts for half of the instances of his name? The most common epithet used with Odysseus is *polymetis*, "of many wiles." It occurs 66 times. Of these, 63 introduce Odysseus for direct speech, 44 of those in the exact formulaic line quoted above that begins Book VIII. Odysseus' most common epithet occurs in very specific, localized contexts: how necessary could it be? Aside from introducing Odysseus for direct speech, his most common epithet occurs but three times in a poem of 12,000 lines.

Another difficulty with Parry's hypothesis is the simple fact that Homer comes to us as a text. Parry almost totally ignores the problem, and Lord evades it by positing an oral-dictated text. Lord imagines "Homer," some preeminent bard, improvising and reciting the long epic to a scribe. However, writing had just re-entered Greece through the Phoenicians, and was a new technology. Writing implements must have been crude; recording massive epic poems in long strings of block capital letters with no spaces must have been a major labor. Indeed, the speed of a chanting oral bard would totally exceed the new technique of writing. The whole basis of the Parry-Lord hypothesis is that the occasion of oral performance, improvising in verse with the pressure of time, creates the need for a formulaic system. But whether a scribe wrote down Homer, or he himself wrote, that specific improvisational pressure would be lifted.

Finally, language is itself an arbitrary system controlled by certain limitations and constrictions, called collectively a "grammar." Language creates meaning through these restraints. Poetry, which opposes itself to normal speech, subjects itself to more constraints, which give it its prosodic or linguistic uniqueness. When we interpret a Shakespeare sonnet, would anyone ever claim that the word at the end of the line is not "semantically relevant" or "intentionally meaningful" because Shakespeare was limited by his need to rhyme? Dr. Samuel Johnson wrote of Pope, "By perpetual practice, language has in his mind a systematical arrangement; having always the same use for words, he had words so selected and combined as to be ready at his call."[2] Perhaps we are closer to Homer here than in Parry.

Scholars have and will continue to argue acrimoniously the many faces of the Homeric Question. But the one aspect of Homer that has met the general agreement of critics and common readers alike is the quality of the poems attributed to him.

Notes

1. Milman Parry, *The Making of Homeric Verse: The Collected Papers of Milman Parry*, ed. Adam Parry. Oxford, 1971.

2. Samuel Johnson, *Life of Pope*.

The Story Behind the Story

No artist of our time can rival Homer in cultural importance and pre-eminence. From him the Greeks derived their core ethics and values; an educated Greek would have huge portions—if not all—of his epic committed to memory. An example from history will give an idea of his centrality: In the sixth century BCE, Athens and Megara were continually contending for control of the important island of Salamis. They agreed to submit the dispute to binding arbitration, and chose a neutral third party. The arbiter ruled in favor of Athens, because the Catalogue of Ships in Book II of the *Iliad* tells that Salamis stationed her ships next to the Athenians. An inconsequential detail of the *Iliad* legislated the outcome of a war.

The Greek historians, looking backward, could see no further than Homer. He was their earliest history; for the later Greeks, the world of Odysseus was their direct past. Techniques of modern archaeology have revealed to us information that could not possibly have been available to Herodotus, and so the relationship of the Homeric epics to the history they purport to describe has been re-evaluated.

Two recent discoveries upended previous approaches to the veracity of Homer's history. The first was a series of digs carried out by an amateur archaeologist named Henrik Schliemann, an avid lover of Homer. Convinced of the essential truth of the tales, he set off (somewhat quixotically) in search of Troy and Mycenae, while less enthusiastic classicists looked on condescendingly, and unearthed several archaeological remnants of Greece. He found ruins in Troy, and upon finding a massive vaulted tomb with a masked corpse in Mycenae, he sent a telegram back to Germany that stated tersely: "I have found the mask of Agamemnon."

Modern dating techniques have shown that the tombs Schliemann found were earlier than when Agamemnon would have lived, but his discoveries totally changed our understanding of early Greek history. Though Schliemann himself did not find it, one ruined city was dug up in Troy that was destroyed violently by fire at the end of the thirteenth century BCE. Most historians believe, or at least find it plausible, that this was the sight immortalized by Homer's poems.

Schliemann's discoveries created many questions. For one, there was no way decisively to connect these early inhabitants of the Peloponnese to the classical Greeks. In 1951, a second groundbreaking discovery was made by an enthusiastic amateur. Thousands of clay tablets had been dug up in Mycenae and in Knossos in which was etched a syllabary script called Linear B. The script went undeciphered and untranslated for many years until Michael Ventris, an architect, decrypted it and showed that it was an early form of Greek. A bridge of language connected the Age of Heroes to the Age of Homer.

The basic picture of early Greece that emerges is this: Around the end of the third millennium BCE, proto-Greeks entered the Peloponnese. They were part of the migrations of several Indo-European peoples at that time, including the Hittites and the Luwians. They probably infiltrated Greece slowly, rather than conquered violently, since many of the place and divinity names are not Indo-European but were borrowed from the original inhabitants.

For the next several hundred years these Indo-European migrants developed into a strong and complex civilization. Mycenae is the most spectacular of the ruins from this time, with its gigantic "Cyclopean" walls and famous Lion's Gate, both still visible today. As it was the most powerful state, and probably responsible for the political and social unity, the entire era from the early second millennium bce until about 1100 BCE is called the Mycenean Age. The general idea of Mycenean Greece that archaeology provides is a period of strong kings with elaborate beaurocracies and palace economies. The Mycenean Age was closer to its contemporary Near Eastern civilizations than to classical Greece. It ended mysteriously at the end of the second millennium. Later Greeks attributed this decline to a "Dorian invasion" from the north, but the true reasons remain obscure.

The most likely date for the composition of the Homeric poems is the late eighth century BCE, so a gap of at least three or four centuries separates Homer from Mycenean times. Which society is depicted in Homer's poems? Dark Age Greece or the Mycenean Age? M. I. Finley aptly reminds us that this "Mycenean Age" is a purely modern construct, and unknown in ancient Greece. Homer's only past was what he had heard from bards before him. There are important differences between the world described by Homer and the Mycenaean world described by archaeology: his arms bear resemblance to the arms of his time; his gods have temples, while in Mycenae there were none; Homer cremates his dead, the Myceneans built huge vaulted tombs.

While Homer stubbornly retains certain archaic practices—such as bronze weapons and war chariots—he mostly portrays his own society, or perhaps that of a century earlier. This is logical for a poet at the end of a long oral tradition: each of the multitude of bards through whom these heroic songs passed, naturally would appropriate, add, modify, or refine them. The poems, then, are amalgams of these various additions and editions, with a few remnants of the actual Mycenean past.

Two social features of Dark Age society in Greece merit mention. The economic, political, and cultural center of any region was the *oikos*, usually translated as the "household," which included the family, the retainers, bards, shepherds, or farmers that clustered around a single royal family. The households of Odysseus, or Nestor, or Menelaus, which we visit in the *Odyssey*, are typical Dark Age *oikoi*. They provided security and sustenance, as well as *mores* and values.

A second central Dark Age institution is denoted by the Greek word *xenia*, which means "guest-friendship" or hospitality. In a world without real cities or centralized authority, and riddled with pirates, all travel depended upon the mutual obligations of *xenia*. In the first Book of the *Odyssey*, Athena visits Ithaka in the guise of Mentor. Telemachus spots him tarrying at the door, and is irked that this *xenos*, guest-friend, has been waiting. He invites him to a generous feast before inquiring his name and home. The appearance of a *xenos*, then, demands certain rights and behaviors. It is the closest thing in the world of Homer to an absolute moral mandate: one of Zeus' epithets is *Zeus xenios*, protector of strangers. Much of the *Odyssey* concentrates on the fulfillment and perversion of the demands of *xenia*.

List of Characters

If Homer's descriptive epithets evoke some quintessential quality of his characters, and ennoble them with the full resonance of tradition, **Odysseus'** epithets continually point to his "manyness": he is *polumetis*, of many (*polu-*) wiles (*metis*), a great cunning intelligence; he is *polumechanos*, and will devise a strategem (*mechanos*) to escape any snare; he is *polutropos*, the man of many turns (*tropos* comprehends the full amphiboly of "turns"—clever turns of mind, figures (tropes) of speech, and the endless actual turns of the wanderer); finally, he is *polutlas*, much-suffering, much-enduring. The repetition of the prefix *polu-* indicates the versatility, adaptability, and even mutability, that equip Odysseus for an unstable world.

Penelope is Odysseus' wife and mother of Telemachus, who resists the blandishments of the suitors during Odysseus' long absence. She is distinguished by her fidelity, prudence, and cleverness.

Telemachus is Odysseus' son, who was a baby when his father departed but is on the threshold of maturity when he returns. The first four books of the *Odyssey*—referred to as the Telemachy—draw Telemachus' voyages in search of his father's *kleos*: a Greek word that means both "fame" and "news." In his search he wins some *kleos* for himself. When his father comes home in disguise, he and Telemachus rout the suitors in collusion.

Eumaeus is the loyal swineherd who tends Odysseus' livestock, and offers him his lodging when Odysseus first lands on Ithaca. Odysseus reveals himself to Eumaeus and enlists his assistance to slaughter the suitors.

Eurycleia is an old servant who nursed Odysseus as a boy, and who, while bathing the disguised Odysseus' feet, joyfully recognizes him by the scar on his thigh.

Laertes is Odysseus' father, who, aching for his son, refuses to come to town. He has forgone his home and bed, sleeping on piles of leaves with the slaves. He and Odysseus are happily reunited at the end of the epic.

Menelaus is the brother of Agamemnon, who commands the Greek army in the *Iliad*, and is the cuckolded husband of Helen. Telemachus visits his luxurious and wealthy palace in Sparta, where Menelaus shares memories of Odysseus and relates his tortuous path home after the Trojan War.

Helen is Menelaus' wife, whose adulterous affair with Paris begins the Trojan War. After the war and several other dalliances she is reunited with Menelaus in Sparta.

Nestor is the oldest commander of the Achaeans assembled for the Trojan War. His counsel is widely respected and heeded by other Greeks, and he often ramblingly reminisces about a more glorious past. He entertains Telemachus at his palace in Pylos in Book III of the *Odyssey*.

Calypso is a goddess who inhabits Ogygia, on the fringes of the world, and detains Odysseus for seven years as he longs for home. She craves to have him as her husband, and offers him immortality with her on Ogygia, but Odysseus refuses her, choosing to return to his mortal wife.

Circe is the daughter of Helios, an enchantress who lives on the westerly island of Aeaea. With her magical drugs she changes Odysseus' men to swine. Odysseus rescues them with an antidote given to him by the god Hermes. Odysseus spends a year with her before being dispatched to consult Teiresias in the underworld.

Achilles is the hero and theme of the *Iliad*, which sings the arousal and resolution of his rage, and its destructive consequences for the Achaeans. Achilles represents a hero of a different type than Odysseus: he is doom-eager, swift, and the best fighter of all the Greeks. He appears twice in the *Odyssey*, in the two *nekuiai*, or underworld scenes. In both, the presentation of Achilles is a locus of confrontation between the two opposed ethical and poetic traditions of the *Iliad* and the *Odyssey*.

Agamemnon is the king and commander of the Greeks in the *Iliad*. When he returns home from Troy, his wife Clytemnestra foully murders him, "like an ox at the trough," because she has had an adulterous affair with Aegisthus. Agamemnon appears in the *Odyssey* in the two *nekuiai*.

Philoetius is a loyal retainer of Odysseus, who helps Odysseus avenge the excesses of the suitors.

Alcinous is King of the Phaeacians, who is Odysseus' host in a long path home. To Alcinous and his enchanted household Odysseus narrates the story of his fabulous wanderings. Alcinous provides Odysseus with a ship and rowers to convey him home.

Arete is the wife of Alcinous.

Nausicaa is the young, unmarried daughter of Alcinous. She is Odysseus' first human encounter after a shipwreck lands him on Scheria. She and Odysseus engage in subtle and unspoken rituals of courtship before she leads him to her parents' house.

Demodocus is the blind bard who entertains the Phaeacians. He sings of the clash between Achilles and Odysseus, the dalliance of Ares and Aphrodite, and the sack of Troy by the Trojan horse. The first and last songs cause Odysseus to draw his mantle over his eyes to hide his tears.

Polyphemus is the giant Cyclops who entraps Odysseus and his men in his cave. Odysseus is able to blind and escape him by the famous ruse of calling himself "Nobody," which prevents Polyphemus' fellow Cyclopes from heeding his cries for help.

Odysseus and his men escape on the fleecy underbellies of the giant's sheep. Polyphemus curses Odysseus to his father Poseidon, god of the sea.

Eurylochus, a member of Odysseus' crew who twice rouses them to mutiny, convinces them to open the bag containing ill-winds, suspects some stashed treasure, and later convinces them to slaughter several of the sun's cattle, this final act of arrogance dooms the crew to death on the sea.

Elpenor is Odysseus' crewman who, during the year sojourn on Circe's isle, drinks too much wine, falls asleep on her roof, and then falls to his death. He is the first shade Odysseus encounters in the underworld, and he begs his master to bury his disfigured corpse.

Teiresias is the blind prophet whom Odysseus consults in the underworld. He warns Odysseus not to harm the cattle of the sun, and tells him that he must one day, after his homecoming, travel far inland, to peoples who do not know the sea, and plant an erect oar in the ground to propitiate Poseidon.

Antinous, the strongest and most prominent of the suitors, leads them to all sorts of unseemly outrages. He is the rudest to the disguised Odysseus, and the first to receive an arrow to the gullet from his bow.

Eurymachus, the second-in-command of the suitors behind Antinoos, grovels pitifully to save his life, but cannot change Odysseus' implacable mind.

Aeolus is King of the drifting island of Aeolia, whom Zeus made warden of the winds. He packages and contains all unfavorable winds in a bull's-hide bag, and gives it to Odysseus. But Odysseus' mutinous crew opens the bag and unleashes contrary winds.

Irus is the public beggar of Ithaca who threatens the disguised Odysseus, and promptly has his jaw shattered.

Theoclymenus is the seer whom Telemachus picks up in Sparta, who prophesies the return of Odysseus and imminent destruction of the suitors.

Melanthius, a perfidious goatherd, sides with the suitors, and happily slaughters Odysseus' livestock for them. He meets a particularly grisly end.

Melantho is the sister of Melanthius, who by wantonly sleeping with suitors disgraces Penelope. She is hanged by Telemachus.

Anticleia, Odysseus' mother, dies grieving for her son. Odysseus sees her in the underworld, and tries three times to embrace her insubstantial form.

Eupeithes, Antinous father, gathers an army of angry kin to avenge the deaths of the suitors. Laertes kills him with a spear throw.

Phemius is the bard in Odysseus' home. He sings of the bitter homecomings of the Achaeans in Book I, and is spared from the general slaughter by Odysseus in Book XXII.

Athena is Odysseus' protector goddess for most of the *Odyssey*. She is both a skilled craftsman and a fierce warrior, and so ambiguously sexed. Her eternal virginity indicates her androgyny, as does the old myth that she was born motherless, from Zeus's head, after he swallowed Metis. This circumstance of birth allies her with *metis*, or cunning intelligence, Odysseus' most essential quality.

Poseidon is the god of the sea who opposes Odysseus' homecoming. Odysseus incurred his wrath by blinding his son,

Polyphemus. Poseidon is the father of the races of the Cyclopes and the Phaeacians.

Zeus, the most powerful divinity in the Greek pantheon, is the only Greek god whose name derives from an ancient Indo-European divinity of the sky. In Homer he is called *pater* (father) and *anax* (king), and his *noos* (mind) is no less than the plot of the epics. In the *Odyssey*, he is a protector of justice and order, and it is by his authority that the suitors' transgressions are punished.

Hermes, the messenger god, holds many liminal or transitional functions: he leads people into and out of sleep, and is the *psychopomp*, the leader-of-souls into the underworld. He assumes the role of Odysseus' protector in the episodes of the wanderings (Books 9–12) while Athena is strangely absent. There, he supplies Odysseus with the antidote to Circe's drugs, the *molu*, that permits him to rescue his men. He is often thought of as a trickster and a cheat, and so is, like Athena, associated with the power of *metis*. He is the only other character in the Homeric corpus besides Odysseus to be called *polytropos*.

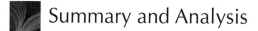

Summary and Analysis

Book I

Andra moi ennepe Mousa, polutropon … (1.1)
Sing in me, Muse, and through me tell the story
Of that man skilled in all ways of contending,
the wanderer … (Fitz. 1–3)[1]

The first word of the *Odyssey* is *andra*: man. Its precursor, the *Iliad*, had sounded a different theme in its first word: *menis*, rage. The word *menis* is typically reserved for divine rage; it is not an emotion that merely smolders, but manifests with violent consequence in the world of action. It is also an emotion that alienates the demigod hero—Achilles—from everything human. The *Iliad* sings the birth and resolution of Achilles' superhuman rage.

The *Odyssey*, however, will sing of *andra*—man. The word is unyoked, at first, to any sort of limiting article or demonstrative, so it is ambiguous: The Greek could equally mean *the* (specific) man, *a* man, or even, more sententiously, Man. The first descriptive epithet that limits this generic, nameless man is *polytropon*—a word on which Fitzgerald lavishes a line and a half of verse. The prefix *poly-* means much or many, and *tropos* means "way" or "turn." Odysseus is the man of many ways, many devices, and the man of many turns, many wandering diversions. So the first characteristic that defines our hero is precisely his adaptability, his fluidity. If in the *Iliad* a hero is a simple, unified beam of action and exposition, the *Odyssey* presents a/the man as something more liquid and shapeless.

The *Iliad* announced its hero's name and patronymic in the very first line: the rage of Achilles, son of Peleus. The *Odyssey's* hero is unnamed until the twenty-first line. The proem of the *Odyssey* is structured like an *ainigma*, a riddle. And the first descriptor, the first hint, of our hero's identity is his *polytropy*: precisely the characteristic that allows for his constant self-concealment and disguise. The Trojan War is over; the simple values of a warrior's life are irrelevant; the commerce of martial *kleos* is closed. And now Odysseus, wandering the margins of the civilized world, will need new abilities to stay alive and find his way home: he will lie, hide, disguise himself, and endure long stretches of anonymity—like the proem itself.

The narration of our story begins with a meeting of the gods on Olympus. Poseidon, "raging cold and rough | against the brave king," is at the earth's verges, absent from the council on Olympus. Zeus begins with a meditation on the story of Aegisthus and Orestes. Aegisthus had seduced Clytemnestra, wife of Agamemnon, while the warrior fought in Troy. On the day of his return, his duplicitous wife conspired with Aegisthus to kill him. Orestes, Agamemnon's son, when he had come of age, avenged his father and killed Aegisthus. Zeus reflects:

My word, how mortals take the gods to task!
All their afflictions come from us, we hear.
And what of their own failings? Greed and folly
Double the suffering in the lot of man. (Fitz. 48–51)

This is the first of multiple references to the bitter *nostos* (homecoming) of Agamemnon. It sets up clear foils to characters in Odysseus' story: Faithful and prudent Penelope is contrasted with the deceitful Clytemnestra; more subtly, Odysseus' strategies of forethought and disguise oppose Agamemnon's open and incautious arrival; and the young and impotent Telemachus is contrasted with Orestes, who valiantly avenged his father. Telemachus has watched for years the suitors devour his patrimony and disgrace his home; will he remain passive, or take up arms, like Orestes?

Moreover, Zeus' speech introduces the theme of human and divine justice, which will relate to the fate of the suitors. It is not the gods who are to blame; humans have both agency and responsibility, and it is their own recklessness (*atasthalia*) which causes them to suffer beyond fate (*hyper moron*). *Atasthalia* implies a voluntary violation of the laws of the god or of men (as opposed to *hamartia*, which is ignorant or involuntary). Odysseus' shipmates, Aegisthus, and ultimately the suitors are all killed by their *atasthalia*—arrogance that incurs recompense.

Athena responds that Aegisthus was indeed justly avenged, and then reminds him of the suffering and detainment of Odysseus. She convinces him that it is time the gods effect his *nostos*, or homecoming, and suggests that Hermes be dispatched to Ogygia to inform Calypso, Odysseus' captor, of the gods' decision, while she goes to Ithaca, to put strength in Telemachus and rouse him to call an assembly of islanders.

Athena comes to Ithaca disguised as Mentes, an old guest-friend of Odysseus. Telemachus is prompt in welcoming her, giving her a share of the feast. Telemachus' kind hospitality contrasts to the wantonness of the suitors around him, who consume the property of an absent man without permission. Athena remarks on Telemachus' resemblance to his father. This invites the rueful reflection:

> Were his death known, I could not feel such pain—
> If he had died of wounds in the Trojan country
> Or in the arms of friends, after the war.
> They would have made a tomb for him, the Akhaians,
> And I should have all honor as his son.
> Instead the whirlwinds got him, and no glory.
>   (Fitz. 281–286)

The pain of Telemachus is the pain of ignorance—that he knows nothing of his father—and of his anonymity—that he may never be known again. The death of a Homeric hero is not mute; it punctuates and closes the life. To die in battle, with a visible tomb to mark that death, assures a well-shaped life and the survival of memory. Instead, thinks Telemachus, Odysseus will not escape the oblivion of an ocean perishing.

Athena tells Telemachus that she has heard that Odysseus is still alive, though detained on an island. She promises he will return soon. Telemachus, hardened by years of unanswered hope, is incredulous. She reminds Telemachus of Orestes, the shining example of a son coming of age by avenging his father, to incite him to bravery. She then suggests to Telemachus a course of action: Call a public assembly to challenge the outrages of suitors, and set off by ship in search of news of his father. As Athena leaves, Telemachus marvels and suspects that Mentes was a god's masquerade.

Among the reprobate suitors, Phemius, the "famous minstrel," begins to sing of the bitter homecomings (*lugroi nostoi*) of the Achaeans. Penelope appears, draped in a full line of epithets, the proper regalia for this epiphany. The descriptive adjective is *periphron*—wise, prudent, circumspect. With tears in her eyes, she requests that Phemius stop that harrowing song. She calls poetry a *thelkterion* (337)—a mode of enchantment. The same word is used for the magic of Circe, Calypso, and the Sirens. Song seduces, allures, beguiles, exercises illicit powers, and here causes Penelope to grieve her absent husband. Telemachus rebukes her: why begrudge the minstrel? he asks. "Poets are not to blame." The allocation of *aitia* (blame or cause) is a concern of this first book of the *Odyssey*: Odysseus is exculpated in the proem, Zeus denies that gods are to blame, and Phemius is not responsible for Penelope's pain.

Telemachus, newly emboldened by the divine visitation, announces to the suitors that their days of irresponsible and profligate feasting are over. The suitors are stung, though remain condescending. The two ringleaders, Antinous and Eurymachus, both reply, skirting the question of their unanswerable conduct.

Telemachus retires, invigorated by new hope, and ponders the path Athena has shown him.

Book II

The form or structure of a literary work can itself be a vehicle of meaning. The events of the *Odyssey* could have been arranged more simply and chronologically, beginning with the sack of Troy by the ruse of the Trojan horse and ending with the completion of Odysseus' *nostos*. But Homer chose to abandon his hero for several books in the beginning, to give earlier episodes nested in songs of other bards, and to let Odysseus himself narrate his fabulous adventures. Homer plunges us *in medias res*, so the story begins in the tenth year of the span it describes (symmetrically to the *Iliad*). Why is the *Odyssey* arranged in this manner?

The first four books of the *Odyssey* are referred to as the Telemachy, because they tell of Telemachus' travels and coming of age. The boy begins irresolute and unassertive before the egregious abuses to his home and name, and then emboldened by Athena, challenges them and goes out to trace his father's footsteps. The Telemachy achieves several important things placed before Odysseus himself is introduced. It establishes the situation at home—that his wife has been faithful, his home is being rapined by men who take him for dead, and his son is maturing so that he may assist him. This is the situation to which Odysseus returns, and would have had to be introduced obliquely and hastily if not narrated in the Telemachy. Several tales are told of Odysseus in the first four books, as we will see, relating to his role in ending the Trojan War, and other heroes give reminiscences of his character. All of these magnify his stature and our expectations before we finally meet him, weeping on a beech, detained by a goddess.

The overarching structure of the Odyssey—beginning *in medias res* on Ithaca, following Odysseus on his final return, and ending again on Ithaca—also has an important emotional effect, noticed by H.D.F. Kitto: Homer "discounts surprise" because he is "concerned with that serious aspect of human existence in which law prevails, in which offense will incur disaster, in which the very nature of things will have the last word."[2] Homer repeatedly foreshadows and hints at the various outcomes of the plot, and this persuades us that the outcomes are natural, and indeed inevitable, because "offense incurs disaster." The supposed "romanticism" of the Odyssey, in his magical wanderings and connubial reunion, is "colouring only," and not "structure and substance." Romanticism depends on pursuing the unknown, and leaving behind all the comforts of the known. Odysseus is impelled by his nostalgia (a desire to return home, make a *nostos*), not by curiosity. The *nostos* is the negation of the adventurous romantic; it is the triumph of the already known.

Book II begins with one of Homer's characteristic and recurring metaphors: dawn spreading her rosy fingers over the sky. Telemachus rises and calls the herald to summon an assembly. When the Ithacans have gathered themselves, Lord Aigyptos, old and sage, leads off with an inquiry into the audacious summoner. No assembly had convened since Odysseus set off for Troy, nineteen years prior.

Telemachus announces that he convened them, and hotly complains of the shameful plundering of his house, perpetrated by men present at the assembly. He is militant and threatening. He begs by Zeus and by Justice that vengeance visit them, and in anger he throws his staff on the ground. Achilles makes an identical gesture in the first book of the *Iliad*: when he defies Agamemnon he "throws his scepter to the ground" (*Il.* 1.245). Both are impetuous and public moments of anger, in the *agora* (meeting-place or assembly).

A silence follows this impassioned and just diatribe. Finally Antinous responds, slyly transferring the responsibility to Penelope. If she would not tarry and delay, the suitors would stop consuming his home. Antinous tells of Penelope's trickery: She agreed to marry one of the suitors, but insisted that she be allowed to finish a funeral shroud for Laertes, Odysseus father. She wove by day, but unraveled by torchlight at night. It took three years for the suitors to uncover this ruse. Dismiss your mother, demands Antinous, or make her marry.

Telemachus says he could never banish his mother against her will; he will not comply. At this, Zeus sends a frightful omen. Two eagles fly above the assembly, wheeling and glaring down up the men, and tear at each other's cheeks and necks with their talons. Halitherses, a man skilled in reading birdflight, interprets the omen: he foretells that Odysseus is near, and he will arrive unrecognized, plotting destruction for those plundering his house. Eurymachus, another suitor, dismisses Halitherses' warning: he refuses to recognize or understand the sign (*sema*). Indeed, the suitors will repeatedly be characterized by their *meconnaisance*: they fail to detect Penelope's ruse, they fail to understand the bird-signs and omens, and finally, fatally, they fail to recognize the disguised Odysseus.

Telemachus petitions the assembly for a ship. Mentor rises to speak; to him Odysseus had given control of his house during his absence. Odysseus was like a gentle father, he reminds the gathered men, how can you perpetrate this revolting insolence? And how can the rest of the citizens passively sit by, in tame content?

Leocritus rises and dismisses Mentor, confident that should Odysseus return, he could never single-handedly best the suitors, who greatly outnumber him. But, he says, let Halitherses and Mentor prepare a ship.

The assembly dissolves, and Telemachus ambles down by the ocean, washing his hands in the water. He prays to the god of yesterday, in despair. Athena answers, and appears in the guise of Mentor. "The son is rare who measures with his father," (ii.292) she reflects. You get provisions ready, she suggests, while she chooses an able ship.

Heeding her, Telemachus returns home to the mocking jeers of the suitors. He escapes to the storeroom to begin provisioning. His trusty nurse Eurycleia aids him, and he demands that his mother not be informed of his plan. Athena weighs down the eyes of the wine-saturated suitors, so that they wander home to bed, and wakes Telemachus to send him on his way.

Book II offers a glimpse into a nascent political institution that will be the hallmark of Greek democracy. For a Greek political thinker like Plato or Aristotle, a sovereign assembly, to which all citizens are entitled to attend, is the foundation of the democratic *polis*. Discussing history in Homer is made difficult by the various strata of Greek history that are combined in his poems. The *Iliad* and *Odyssey* are a kind of haphazard amalgam of customs and practices of several hundred years of Greek society. But the assembly scene, though surely not democratic, shows in embryonic form commitment to oratory and persuasion that would characterize later Greek political institutions.

Book III

Another image of dawn begins this book. The sun springs up from the "flawless, brimming" sea, into a "brazen heaven," to shine upon "grain-giving earth." The previous book began with the image of dawn's rose-red fingers moving over the horizon. Homer's metaphors of dawn are among the most popular and memorable to new readers. There is certainly, in these images, a freshness, a majestic simplicity, which is surpassing. No amount of quarreling between professional Homerists about whether formulae are "intentionally meaningful" or "original" could efface their beauty. Homer speaks to that nucleus of childhood within, which no amount of commerce with the world can smother. A critic has written, "An excess of childhood is the germ of a poem." Nowhere else is the energy of childhood so abundant as in Homer.

Telemachus and his men arrive at Pylos, against this auroral backdrop. They sacrifice many bulls to the earth-shaker, Poseidon. Athena approaches Telemachus, who has held back in disembarking, and encourages him: No shyness now, ask for tidings of your father.

They come upon Nestor, enthroned in his palace among family and retainers. Nestor was the oldest and wisest of the Greeks who set out for Troy. To his seasoned judgment the Greeks directed their most vital decisions. Nestor asks Telemachus and Athena to join in their libations to Poseidon.

They all feast their fill before Nestor asks their stories: Who are you, *xenoi*? Are you here on some business? Or are you marauding pirates, wandering over the sea?

Before Telemachus answers, Homer inserts an interesting parenthetical remark:

"Athena gave Telemachus confidence in his mind, so that he could ask about his absent father, and have good *kleos* (fame) among men" (76–78). *Kleos* is the attainment of the Homeric hero that expands him (or her)[3] beyond the limits of life; it is for *kleos aphthiton*—imperishable fame—that Achilles chooses a short lifetime over a safe return. Telemachus' small voyage, by Athena's design, will initiate him into this economy of *kleos*. One critic has argued that simply exposure to Pylos and Sparta,

32

and to the old heroes of the Trojan War, will give Telemachus *kleos*. But in addition to acquiring *kleos* by osmosis, as it were, Telemachus' search for news of his father will begin his own quest of revenge: if Odysseus lives, he can wait to avenge the suitors together with him; if he has died, he will shoulder the burden alone, like Orestes.[4] Telemachus tells Nestor that he is the son of Odysseus, and that he has come for news of his father. Not knowing how or where his father died, Telemachus feels the bitterness of ignorance:

> As to the other men who fought that war,
> We know where each one died, and how he died,
> But Zeus allotted my father death and mystery.
> (Fitz. 94–96)

Odysseus' unknown and unseen death lacks the clear meaningfulness of a heroic death. Achilles died on the battlefield, and his crematory fires radiated an appropriate consummation of a heroic life. In the first book of Herodotus, Solon reminds Croesus that one cannot judge a life until its end in death. A death of anonymity threatens to swallow Odysseus in eternal meaninglessness, like an unfinished sentence.

Nestor reminisces on the miseries the Achaeans endured in Troy. After Troy had fallen, Menelaus and Agamemnon, two brothers, quarreled over when to leave for home, the latter urging that they delay so as to sacrifice to Athena. The Achaeans thus were divided in their various *nostoi*. Odysseus had left with Nestor, we learn, though he decided to put back, in order to please king Agamemnon. Nestor briefly charts the *nostoi* of a catalogue of heroes, ending with the sad fate of Agamemnon, and the just revenge of his son.

Telemachus responds that Orestes will indeed have "broad *kleos* and be a song to future generations" (204), and if the gods granted him the *dynamis*—the potency—he would avenge the arrogant suitors.

Telemachus asks for more information on the slaying of Agamemnon, and more precisely, why did his brother,

Menelaus, not protect him? Nestor explains that he had begun his homeward voyage with Menelaus, who split off when grounded to bury a crewman who had died suddenly. Menelaus was blown by a tempest down to Egypt, where he tarried, accumulating money in sea traffic. He was in Egypt for the perfidy of Aegisthus and Clytemnestra. Nestor urges Telemachus to visit Menelaus in Lacedaemon, as he may have more information on his father.

Athena urges all to turn their thoughts to bed. More sacrifices are made to Poseidon, and Nestor insists that his *xenoi* stay in beds in his palace. Athena declines, and her sudden disappearance convinces all onlookers that she is immortal. Telemachus agrees to spend the night.

Another rosy-fingered dawn appears, and then an elaborate description of a sacrifice. Telemachus and Peisistratus, Nestor's son, set off in a chariot furnished by Nestor. They reach Lacedaemon on the second day, after sundown.

Book IV
They find Menelaus hosting a double wedding feast, marrying off his daughter to the heir of Achilles, and his tall scion, Megapenthes, to Alector's daughter. In happiness they feast, while a minstrel harps and sings, and acrobats tumble and flip around. The two strangers at the door are met by Eteoneus, a squire of Menelaus. Should we receive them? he asks, or make them move on?

Menelaus gently reprimands him: You are talking like a foolish child, he says. "Could we have made it home again … if other men had never fed us, given us lodging?" (iv.36–38) The safety and very possibility of travel depends on the hospitality of strangers. As Menelaus warmly welcomes Telemachus, an exemplar of *xenia*, two perversions of *xenia* motivate the action of the epic: the suitors, guests in the palace of Odysseus, uninvited, plunder and abuse the opportunities of the house. Meanwhile Odysseus himself is marooned on an island, the *xenos* of a goddess who craves him for her own. She has detained him against his will.

Telemachus and Peisistratus enter the palace and are stunned by the glittering wealth on display. Maidservants bathe and clothe them, and they sit beside Menelaus. Their plates are heaped high with food, and their cups brimmed with wine. When they have eaten their fill, Telemachus marvels to Peisistratus that with endless treasure aglow, the halls of Zeus himself must look like Menelaus'. Menelaus overhears; he wisely reminds the young Telemachus that no mortal can vie with the gods. "What pleasure can I take, then, being lord | over these costly things?" Death cuts short the life of every mortal; man is an ephemeral creature, "the dream of a shadow," as the lyric poet Pindar will phrase it in two centuries. How, Menelaus continues, can he enjoy these earthly possessions when his brother was so foully murdered? He would give them up to see his friends safe home from Troy. There is one companion he misses more than the others: Odysseus, man of woe. He is pained by this absence, and by his own consequent ignorance. He does not even know if he is alive.

At this, Telemachus cannot beat down the pangs for his unknown father, and his weeping behind his cloak betrays him to Menelaus. Helen enters, with her train, and immediately comments on the likeness of Telemachus and Odysseus. When Peisistratus confirms that they have indeed discerned correctly, Menelaus ebulliently recalls his love for Odysseus, with a poignancy that brings all to tears:

> A twinging ache of grief rose up in everyone,
> And Helen of Argos wept, the daughter of Zeus,
> Telemakhos and Menelaos wept,
> And tears came to the eyes of Nestor's son ...
> (Fitz. 196–199)

The scene is a motif in Homer: raw grief cedes to a meal. Menelaus says: "Come, we'll shake off this mourning mood of ours | and think of supper." (iv.228–229) Just as we are moved by the universality of grief, so also are we moved by the simple, pleasurable universal of eating. Battered by bereavements, distanced from a will to live, food is the instrument that re-engages us to life.

As a meal is spread before them, Helen slips into the wine a drug, a *pharmakon*, to quiet grief, and bring "sweet oblivion" from painful memory. The opiate was supplied her in Egypt. The later books of the *Odyssey* will explore the necessary cognitive kinship that underlies love, and call in *homophrosyne*—like-mindedness. This quality finds its apotheosis in Odysseus and Penelope. Helen's *pharmakon*, which induces forgetfulness, and so suppresses the function of the mind, indicates some tension or illness that needs to be artificially softened. Perhaps the mental wounds inflicted by Helen's legendary infidelities can never be healed, only numbed.

Helen and Menelaus reminisce, exchanging stories about Odysseus. Helen recalls Odysseus' brilliant disguise, when, in the tattered clothes of a beggar, he entered Troy unnoticed to scout it out. She alone recognized him—though in his cunning he avoided her. Finally, unmasked, he slaughtered many Trojans on his departure. While the women wailed, says Helen, she rejoiced inwardly: for she "repented | the mad day Aphrodite | drew me away from my dear fatherland ..." Helen has given a rather bleak depiction of love, or, more precisely, *eros*. Eros is a form of *ate*: madness and blindness.

Menelaus tells all that no man could rival Odysseus for steadiness of heart. While all the Greek heroes were hidden, packed inside the Trojan horse, Helen walked round it, calling out to all the fighters in the voice of their wives. Odysseus fought all down, despite their longing to reply, and clamped his hand over the weak mouth of Anticlus before he could betray them. Telemachus is saddened that these valors could not protect his father from death.

The heroes awake as another rosy-fingered dawn brightens the earth. Menelaus asks Telemachus why he rode "the sea's broad back" to Sparta. Telemachus tells of the situation in his home—his mother besieged by arrogant men consuming his patrimony—and asks for news of his father.

Menelaus narrates his own story: Being too scant in sacrifices to the gods, he was detained in Egypt. Becalmed and starving, he asks advice of Eidothea, who is the daughter of Proteus, the Old Man of the Sea. She explains how to subdue and question her father, who knows all things. From Proteus Menalaus hears of the *nostoi* of other heroes. Ajax arrogantly taunted the sea, and was crushed by Proseidon's violent waters. *Hubris* against the gods incurred disaster. Menelaus first learns of the death of his brother, Agamemnon, whom treacherous Aegisthus tricked: he lay out a feast when the great king returned, only foully to do him in, "like an ox felled at the trough." The simile captures the indignity of this death, which does not befit so great a hero as Agamemnon. Proteus then tells of Odysseus, marooned at sea, detained by the goddess Calypso.

Last of all Menelaus learns his own destiny. He has married a daughter of Zeus, so he gains admittance to the Isle of the Blest. Proteus describe the happy fate:

… the gods intend you for Elysion
with golden Rhadamanthos at the world's end,
where all existence is a dream of ease.
Snowfall is never known there, neither long
Frost of winter, nor torrential rain,
But only mild and lulling airs from Ocean
Bearing refreshment for the souls of men …
(Fitz. 599–605)

A critic named William Anderson has questioned whether this Elysian future is really desirable. Menelaus has told Telemachus that a life among his Olympian possessions, a life of sensuality, cannot give him happiness—he is already living, miserably, in a human Elysium. The story each spouse tells of Troy, moreover, is in conflict with the other. The ostensible subject of Helen's story is Odysseus, but it is really about herself. She recognized him; she rejoiced; she repented what she had done. And we can hardly believe her plea of repentance: she would still have another dalliance with Deiphobus, and would aid the Trojans in the very story that Menelaus tells. We can only imagine the rage and frustration of Menelaus, pent up in the Trojan horse, as his wife tries to seduce out all of the heroes. "The two conflicting memories of Troy expose the smouldering emotions that threaten the outward calm of this prosperous scene in Sparta."[5] The easy night in Sparta is dependent upon a drug to hide their past. "Against this background in Sparta, Elysium is not so enticing."[6] In fact, Elysium has similarities to Ogygia, where Odysseus is detained: both are loveless yet sensual eternities.

The narrative shifts back to Ithaca, to the suitors blithely competing, gaming away the time. In the *Iliad*, games are a temporary diversion from meaningful heroic action. By contrast, lazy gaming is the suitors' primary activity. Noemon, who had lent Telemachus his ship, unwittingly reveals to the suitors that Telemachus has gone voyaging. They convene, baffled and hostile. Antinous conspires to trap and kill him at sea.

Medon, who had heard the suitors conspiring, runs up to tell Penelope. Her knees go slack with grief. She cries; she is unable to speak. After a long while she forces out: "Why did he go? Must he, too, be forgotten?" (iv.761). Once again the pain of death is a matter of amnesia.

Eurycleia, her trusty nurse, advises her to bathe and pray to Athena. The suitors, meanwhile, load and arm a ship. They moor it offshore.

While Penelope sleeps, Athena sends her a dream messenger, in the guise of Iphthime, Penelope's sister. The dream-vision assures her that Telemachus will return unharmed, and that Athena is by her side. Penelope asks about Odysseus; there is no reply.

The suitors wait in ambush for Telemachus.

Book V

The most straightforward approach is this: The Greeks had a tragic conception of life. They understood both the immense potential of the human, and the inevitable gloom of mortality. Locked in this circumstance, the Homeric hero will compete for the only immortality available to him: *kleos aphthiton*, imperishable fame. That is a consolation and bulwark against the horror of death. Immortality of this kind is intellectual, metaphorical: the hero will not breathe, or think, or sense. In the absence of the reality of immortality, a hero will settle for its metaphor. This is contradicted by Odysseus: when Calypso offers him literal immortality, the life of a god, he chooses the metaphor over the truth. He chooses death and figural immortality (his song), *kleos aphthiton*, over its reality. He chooses humanity—with its imperfections, limitations, and tragedy.

> *Nostos*, his return; *gyne*, Penelope, his wife; Ithaka, his homeland, son, aging father faithful companions; and then *thanein*, to die. These are all those things toward which Odysseus' power to love, his nostalgic desire, and his *pothos* yearn because he has wearied of Kalypso and has refused a non-death that is also a non-life.[7]

Immortality could only be purchased by relinquishing his family, his name, his memory, and all of his epic achievements; so, he refuses it.

Dawn arises from her couch, and the gods convene on Olympus. The assembly of the gods that begins Book V resembles very closely the assembly of Book I. Critics who would cheerfully apply the Analyst scalpel to Homer point to this needless repetition as evidence that the Telemachy is a later interpolation, while the *Odyssey* proper begins here. This opinion neglects two general points about Homer: First, questions of composition notwithstanding, the Homeric poems were intended to be delivered orally. The magnitude of the poems necessitates that performances be divided. We can easily imagine that the Telemachy is a convenient segment for a day's performance, and that picking up the thread again in Book V required some re-introducing of themes and characters. Second, Homer never employs the narrative nuance of giving simultaneous events. Synchrony is not in his repertoire; instead, he is constantly linearizing. We should not expect Homer to introduce the Odysseus strand in a massive "meanwhile" construction.

Athena reminds Zeus that Odysseus continues to grieve in thralldom to the nymph, Calypso, with no means of faring homeward. Zeus commands Hermes, the messenger of the gods, to announce to Calypso that the gods have resolved to effect the hero's *nostos*. Hermes courses over the sea to Ogygia, and finds Calypso by a fragrant fire, weaving and singing. Around her, buds, greenery, and springs abound in idyllic splendor. Odysseus sits apart, groaning.

Hermes tells Calypso of the gods' decision. Calypso effuses her grief, hating the gods for their jealousy, that immortal and mortal flesh should mingle. Broken, she complies.

Calypso goes to find Odysseus, who sits scanning the sea through teary eyes. There is an important nuance in the Greek description of Odysseus that comes here, often overlooked in translation: "His sweet life was ebbing away, as he grieved for his return, for the nymph no longer pleased him" (152–153). The word *ouketi*—"no longer"—implies that she once did please him, and, indeed, pleased him enough that the thought of his unappeased *nostos* did not sting. Ultimately, this pleasure and isolation began to undermine the self he had fought so long to attain.

Calypso tells Odysseus he is free, but offers him immortality with her. Immortality had long before lost its appeal with his extinguished sensuality. She has offered not eternal life, but an eternal death-in-life, in which all of his past achievements, loves, and aspirations lose their meaning. He declines.

Odysseus builds a ship, and in five days is on the open sea, navigating by the stars. After seventeen days of solitary seafaring, Scheria is visible, like a "rough shield of bull's hide of the sea" (Fitz. 291).

But his easy passage is foiled. Poseidon spots him, and conjures a tremendous storm. Odysseus is battered by gales and foaming surges. He laments that he soon will be swallowed by the ocean, and wishes a soldier's death. We have seen the sea function as a trope for the forces of anonymity; in this light, the simile quoted just above assumes fresh meaning: land and civilization are a "shield," a defense, against the endless sea.

A Nereid, a sea-nymph, Ino, visits Odysseus, giving advice and a protective cloak. Odysseus at first disobeys, following a course that to his discernment seems best, but circumstances compel him to follow the nymph. Athena quiets the winds, but for two days and two nights he drifts on the swollen waves. Then he spots land:

> What a dear welcome thing life seems to children
> whose father, in the extremity, recovers
> after some weakening and malignant illness:
> his pangs are gone, the gods have delivered him.
> So dear and welcome to Odysseus
> the sight of land, of woodland, on that morning.
> (Fitz. 411–416)

His elation is short-lived; he soon hears the roar of sea on rock. He clasps a crag as a billow launches him forward; its ebb tears him away, scraping off skin from his hands. He spots an inlet stream and floats into the quiet water. He prepares a bed among the leaves:

> A man in a distant field, no hearthfires near,
> will hide a fresh brand in his bed of embers
> to keep the spark alive for the next day;
> so in the leaves Odysseus hid himself,
> while over him Athena showered sleep
> that his distress should end, and soon, soon.
> In quiet sleep she sealed his cherished eyes.
> (Fitz. 513–519)

Book VI

An island that offers nothing but the monotony of sensuality, that grants a possibility of *kleos*-conferring competition, and that shields hardship, is both a grave and a womb. Calypso's island can be likened to eternal death: the very name "Calypso" comes from the Greek *kalyptein*, which means to cover or conceal, and is a common Homeric metaphor for death ("a cloud of death covered him"). But Ogygia can also be a pre-natal oblivion. As Odysseus leaves this island, where he exists without identity, he undergoes symbolic birth. Odysseus emerging naked from his cocoon of leaves, where he spent the night like a *sperma pyros*, "the seed of a fire," reinforces our sense of birth.

With birth inevitably comes hardship, but without hardship there is no manner of assuming an identity. The identity of the Homeric hero is *agonistic*—that is, based on competition. In the motionless torpor of a life on Ogygia, where he cannot strive to be best, the hero is not alive. There is a pun on Odysseus' name in Book V that will aid our understanding of this. When Ino first speaks to Odysseus, she says:

O forlorn man, I wonder
why the Earthshaker, Lord Poseidon, holds
this fearful grudge ... (Fitz. 350–353)

The verb of Poseidon's anger is *odyssein*, "to be wroth against." Autolycus, Odysseus' grandfather, named him from this verb (see Book XIX). To render the effect cumbersomely in English, we might say: Poseidon is "odysseusing" Odysseus. The god of the sea is wroth against him, he is battering him on the sea, sending him woes, and impeding an easy *nostos*. But Odysseus, symbolically born after leaving the womblike comforts of Ogygia, is *becoming Odysseus*. Poseidon "odysseuses" him: sends him trouble, and gives him back his name.[8]

As Odysseus sleeps among the olive trees, Athena appears to the beautiful young princess of Scheria named Nausicaa. Nausicaa is like a goddess in looks, prudent and virginal: the ideal *parthenos* (unmarried maiden). Athena announces to Nausicaa that her maidenhood must end; she must bring her linens down to the fresh springs to wash in the morning.

Nausicaa and her attendant maids wash their clothes and bathe in the clean water. Then they eat a picnic lunch and play at ball. An errant toss rouses Odysseus, slumbering nearby. Odysseus leaves the bush, covering himself with an olive branch, "like a mountain lion ... with burning eyes—who

prowls among the herds or flocks, or after game..."
(vi.140–143). While her maids scatter into hiding, frightened
of the burly and brine-covered visitor, Nausicaa stands to meet
him. Odysseus ponders—do I grasp the maidens knees in
supplication? Or just use "honeyed" speech? He decides on
the latter, and devotes the famed Odyssean intelligence to
flirtatious banter. "Mistress, please: are you divine or mortal?...
Never have I laid eyes on equal beauty | in man or woman. I
am hushed indeed.... I stand in awe so great | I cannot take
your knees" (Fitz. 161–181).

When Nausicaa and her attendants begin to play they
throw off their veils: this is an ambiguous gensture, since the
veil in Homer is the emblem of modesty and chastity.
Odysseus, when he awakes, compares their voices to nymphs:
seductive and sexualized creatures. They are also compared to
Artemis and her attendants, enternally chaste virgins. This
confused symbolism exposes a confused drama of sexual
awakening in Nausicaa: "the poet suggests the confusion
attendant upon adolescent sexuality between innocent modesty
and a certain forwardness which is only dimly recognized, if at
all, by Nausicaa herself."[9] With its sexual suggestions, the
moment is threatening to both Nausicaa and Odysseus: young
maidens blithely playing are traditional targets of rape in Greek
literature,[10] and the stranger has just been compared to a
hungry lion. For Odysseus, meanwhile, Nausicaa threatens to
stagnate or end his quest for home, like Circe and Calypso, the
other seductive females he has encountered.

Nausicaa offers him food, drink, and bath. He wanders off
to bathe, insisting that his nakedness not besmirch the eyes of
young *parthenoi*. He rinses off and anoints himself with oil, and
Athena lavishes beauty on him, making him seem massive and
glowing. At his reappearance the *parthenoi* are all aflutter,
admiring his godlike visage. They offer food, which he eats
ravenously, having fasted on the open sea for two days.

Nausicaa offers Odysseus passage to the town, and to the
palace of her parents. But she tells him to tarry behind her
wagon, lest ogling townsmen think they are to be married,
shamefully flouting her parents. This is her subtle flirtatious

rejoinder to Odysseus' flattery. As they make their way toward town, Odysseus prays to Athena that he may find love and mercy among the Phaeacians. Athena hears him, though Poseidon "smolders on."

When Odysseus first speaks to Nausicaa, tempering coquettishness with a worldly wisdom, he tells her: "The best thing in the world [is] a strong house, held in serenity, where man and wife agree." The best thing is a home where man and wife are *homophron*, literally, "with the same mind," or "sympathetic." The word denotes generally a kind of psychic harmony that prevails in the well-ordered *oikos* (household). It presents love in marriage as the joint possession of a single composite mind. Odysseus' long absence has fractured this consonance, and the *telos* of his voyage home is to reestablish this broken *homophrosyne*. In the end, a *nostos* is the attainment of a psychological state, not a phenomenal one. The pain of the separated family is ignorance: not knowing the location, the health, or the fidelity of the loved one. Odysseus' nostalgia is made painful by his ignorance; and the real threat to his *nostos* is amnesia, the forgetting of his voyage home. We will see later that the Lotus flower, and the song of the Sirens, are all fundamentally cognitive threats: they threaten *lethe*, forgetfulness of home. Returning home, Odysseus will repair his broken knowledge, and memory will triumph over amnesia. Then he may attain the psychical state of being home.

Book VII
As instructed by Nausicaa, Odysseus delays and prays in the grove. As he enters the city, Athena showers a mist upon him, so that none see him. Athena disguises herself as a small girl, who leads Odysseus to the palace, giving him a brief account of the royal lineage. She praises Queen Arete for her equity, and the respect she commands.

Odysseus gazes upon the resplendent palace, and the fecund vineyards and orchards that surround it. Entering the great hall, sliding unnoticed past the feasters within, he grabs Arete's knees in supplication. Echeneus, the eldest of the

Phaeacians, "understanding the wisdom of old," speaks up: Give the man a seat of honor; respect your *xenos*. Odysseus joins the feast. Eying his visitor's aspect, Alcinous broods that this man might be a god.

No, not a god, Odysseus assures Alcinous. All earth and mortal. And now my belly bids me eat.

Arete, noticing Odysseus' clothing, asks where he got it. We may infer there is some suspicion in that question. Odysseus tells of his detainment on Ogygia, cold lover of the immortal nymph. "In my heart I never gave consent." He was wracked by Poseidon, he explains, and he first met Nausicaa. She, beautiful yet prudent, had offered him clothing.

Alcinous, sensing nobility in his visitor, and reflecting that he is surely not of mean descent, offers Odysseus Nausicaa's hand, and a rich kingdom on Scheria. Should he not desire this, Alcinous promises conveyance home the next day. Odysseus prays exultantly. All retire to bed.

A common opinion among Attic comedians and philosophers, and among Alexandrian critics, was that Odysseus was an indulgent glutton. It did not befit a hero to answer to the base urgings of his offals; no hero is more sensitive to the mandates of belly than Odysseus. Pope called the Odyssey the "eatingest of epics," and, indeed, almost every narrative situation involves a meal.

When Alcinous suggests that Odysseus may be a god, Odysseus is quick to assure him that he is human. "I [am] all of earth and mortal nature." And, as if to verify his humanity, to give the watchword of his mortality, Odysseus manifests cravings of belly (*gaster*):

> "You will indulge me if I finish dinner—?...
> There's no part
> of man more like a dog than brazen Belly,
> crying to be remembered—and it must be—
> when we are mortal weary and sick at heart;
> and that is my condition. yet my hunger
> drives me to take this food, and think no more
> of my afflictions. Belly must be filled. (Fitz. 330–337)

W. B. Stanford has argued that there is no better indication of Odysseus' unconventionality as a Homeric hero than his attitude toward food. An episode in the *Iliad* clarifies this unconventionality. After Achilles agrees to rejoin the fighting, having redirected his rage toward Hector with the death of his close friend Patroclus, he is ferally eager for slaughter. He is so crazed for war that he refuses food and drink, and commands the assembled Achaeans to do the same. Odysseus objects; he is far more prudent, reminding all that to fight on an empty stomach is disadvantageous. Achilles' rejection of food is something superhuman. Odysseus' insistence is simply good sense.

Odysseus has human attachments. The other great Homeric heroes die unhappily, living short, fiery lives with a young death. Achilles, raging and mourning his friend, refuses food as a rebellion against his very mortality. Achilles, as he neglects food, is tragic but deceived about his condition as human, though there is a certain consoling sublimity in that deception. Odysseus is frank and realistic; he would never be so childish as to pout at mortality. But his realism requires both an acquiescence in the belly, in death, and the realization that food has an important physiological function.

Sublime heroism disregards belly, but even the fieriest hero of all returns to food as he reengages to human life. In Book XXIV, Achilles and Priam share a meal which emblemizes their shared grief, shared humanity, and healing. Odysseus shares many meals in his "eatingest of epics," and all remind us of that pleasant physiological necessity which attaches him to earth.

Book VIII

Alcinous, beneath dawn's fingers, calls an assembly, and commands the best seamen to ready a ship. The elders, meanwhile, should make ready more a day of feasting.

The assembly dissolves and processes into the great house of Alcinous. A herald leads in the blind bard, Demodocus,

...The man of song
whom the Muse cherished; by her gift he knew
the good of life, and evil—
for she who lent him sweetness made him blind.
   (Fitz. 67–70)

The man, robbed of his eyes, who thereby gains a second inner, or spiritual, sight is a common motif in Greek literature. The bard Demodocus is the earliest extant specimen in that trend; he may also be the archetype for later imaginings of what Homer may have been.

When hunger and thirst are appeased in the gathered feasters, the Muse moves the minstrel to sing the glorious deeds of men. He sings of a quarrel between Odysseus and Achilles, at which Agamemnon smiles inwardly, knowing it is a harbinger of an imminent Greek victory. We never learn the cause or details of the clash from Homer.

The quarrel sung by Demodocus is a reminder of a larger thematic clash that rings through the whole poem: who is the best of the Achaeans, *aristos Akhaion*? Odysseus or Achilles? The Greeks never awarded a silver or bronze at the Olympic Games; there is only one who is *aristos*. Odysseus and Achilles exemplify two different modes of *agon* (competition). Odysseus competes with his *metis* (mind), while Achilles competes with his *bie*, strength.

Who are their opponents? Though ostensibly the Homeric hero vies with other soldiers, the real opponent of their *agon* is death itself. The Homeric poems present man's various attempts to subdue or outwit death, or at least the apprehension of death, whether by spear, by song, or by clever ruse. Achilles, in his rage, is the sublime apotheosis of the warrior; he nonetheless goes down to death young. Rebelling against death with one's *bie* is self-destructive. Odysseus is the hero of *metis*; he lives a long life and dies in the comfort of his fatherland. He also deals death the sharpest blow it can receive: he rejects immortality, and willingly invites its sting. The injustice of death is its blind inevitability; Odysseus outwits it, overcomes it in mind, by accepting its centrality in human meaning.

In more practical affairs as well, it is ultimately the guile (*metis*) of the Trojan horse, authored by Odysseus, that wins the Trojan War, and not force (*bie*).

As Demodocus sings the quarrel of heroes, Odysseus draws his cloak over his brow to hide his tears. His tears flow unnoticed by all except Alcinous, who relieves Odysseus by cutting off the bard and encouraging all to go to the fields to compete in boxing, wrestling, jumping, and running.

Odysseus lays low amid the athletics, until a contentious and impetuous youth challenges and insults him. He grabs the heaviest discus and hurls it well beyond the nearest competitor. He shouts out a general challenge.

Alcinous calms the situation, diverting all to Demodocus and his harp. The bard plucks and intones the dalliance of Ares and Aphrodite, or the forbidden mingling of lust and war, and their apprehension by Hephaestus. The song begins in indirect speech, but melts gradually into direct speech. Homer's song, at that moment, is in limbo between a detached retelling and the literal assumption of Demodocus' song.

Alcinous requests that the wealthiest Phaeacian lords bring gold and fresh-laundered tunics to send off their distinguished guest. All make ready for the evening feast.

Odysseus is lavishly bathed and clothed by the serving-women, and then joins the festivity. As he sits to eat, he carves a piece of meat for Demodocus: "All men owe honor to poets." Odysseus tells Demodocus that his vivid eloquence gives the impression that he was physically present at the sufferings he describes. Odysseus clearly privileges presence as a source of vividness. Demodocus, however, is blind. His physicality of description is a mode of representation, since his only sight is the inside.

Demodocus sings of the ruse of the Trojan horse, and the sack of Troy. Again Odysseus wraps his cloak over his eyes, to shield from sight his tears. He weeps, Homer tells us,

the way a wife mourns for her lord
on the lost field where he has gone down fighting...
At the sight of the man panting and dying there,
she slips down to enfold him, crying out;
then feels the spears, prodding her back and shoulders,
and goes bound into slavery and grief.
Piteous weeping wears away her cheeks:
So did Odysseus let fall pitiful tears ...
  (Fitz., slightly modified, 562–570)

Here is an instance of a Homeric simile that takes on a narrative momentum in its elaboration, until intersecting again with the main narrative. The simile is somewhat unexpected: comparing Odysseus, a brawny warrior, to a weeping woman? Homer always seems to concern himself with what is most universal in the human: to conjure Odysseus' overwhelming grief, common experience to all, he will not confine himself to narrow categories of analogy.

Alcinous, noticing the weeping again, more forcefully inquires his name. Now Odysseus will spin his own narrative, and hold his listeners spellbound as he recounts his wanderings. But Alcinous gives a final reflection: "Gods fashion destruction, so that it might be a song for men to come." Song is self-justifying, and so justifies the grief that inspires it.

Book IX
  Odysseus replies:

There is no boon in life more sweet, I say,
than when summer joy holds all the realm,
and banqueters sit listening to a harper
in a great hall, by rows of tables heaped
with bread and roast meat, while a steward goes
to dip up wine and brim your cups again.
Here is the flower of life, it seems to me! (Fitz. 5–11)

This passage was oft quoted by moralizers who wanted to impugn Odysseus for gluttony. But food in the epic serves not as an object of greed, but as a mode rejoining or reengaging the world after great sufferings or misfortunes have alienated someone. By sharing food, the stranger (or the estranged) is made familiar.

Now, his *kleos* ringing through the great hall from the strings of Demodocus, as if he were a great hero of a distant past, Odysseus reveals to all his name:

> I am Odysseus, Laertes' son, known for my guile
> to all men. My *kleos* reaches the heavens. (19–20)

Like a ghost from a past where men were stronger, and glory was a possibility to be got by excellence, Odysseus makes his epiphany. This is the only time in all of Homer that a hero refers to his *kleos* in the present tense, as something already present and accomplished. He begins to narrate his story, beginning from when he plundered the city of Troy, and moving ever homeward, for "Where can a man find sweetness to surpass his own home?" (Fitz. 38).

Odysseus' first exploit after the war is to sack the Cicones, exterminating all the men, plundering the wealth, and enslaving women and children. This is pure piracy, but piracy, it seems, was a legitimate and even honorable profession in the world of Odysseus.

Zeus rouses a storm against the ships as they round Cape Malea; a current and gale spirit them out to sea. They drift for nine days; this is their passage into surreality.

On the tenth day, they touch the coast of the Lotus-Eaters. The islanders harvested and ate an opiate plant, that drugged men into such addiction that they would refuse to leave the isle. Whoever ate the honey-sweet fruit "forgot his *nostos*." Here is an explicit link of *nostos* to memory, and the failed *nostos* to amnesia. Memory is Odysseus' only fragile link to his home, and the only material from which to rebuild old relationships, so its erasure ends his journey. Odysseus drives the men who tried the fruit of the Lotus to the ship, as they wail, and lashes them down.

The next coast they touch is the land of the Cyclopes. Of all the episodes in the *Odyssey*, Odysseus' encounter with the one-eyed giant may be the most well known. The plot of the episode is simple, its own self-contained parable: Odysseus out of curiosity wanders into the cave of a giant man, Polyphemus, bringing along several men. The giant returns, and closes the mouth of the cave with a boulder too massive for a normal man to lift. For his dinner, the giant eats two of Odysseus' men, and threatens that the rest of them shall be future dinners. Odysseus then devises a clever stratagem for their escape. He tells the giant that his name is Nobody, and shapes an olive branch into a lance. That night he gets the giant drunk on some liquor he brought along, and as Polyphemus snores, he heats up his poker in the fire. He jams the hot point into the giant's eye, blinding him, and when his fellow Cyclopes hear the screams and racket, they ask what the matter is. "Nobody did this to me!" shouts the giant in agony. "Well, if nobody did this, we'll return to bed," say his peers. To escape the cave, Odysseus and his men cling to the fleecy underbellies of Polyphemus' sheep as they go out to graze. Odysseus taunts the giant and announces his real name as they sail off. The utterance of the proper name allows Polyphemus to curse him to Poseidon.

Amidst more general thematic concerns of the *Odyssey*, we can see in this episode the ultimate perversion of *xenia*, the obligations of guest-friendship. To protect and accept strangers is a mandate enforced by Zeus himself, and all the major actors of the *Odyssey* in some way respond to this compulsion: Nestor, Menelaus, and Telemachus are exemplary, whereas the suitors ravish Odysseus' possessions uninvited, Kalypso detains her guest against his will, and the Cyclops eats his own guests. Odysseus several times comments that the Cyclopes do not till any fields, that they are lawless, each man legislating his own home, and that they do not fear the gods. Lacking these three fundaments of civilized life, they neglect the basic moral obligations that accompany them.

The episode is also a mythic and archetypal parable of *metis* defeating *bie*, or mind defeating might. All the victories of the *Odyssey* are won with mind, and even the Trojan War itself (the slaughter of the suitors, which seems to be the most Iliadic achievement of Odysseus, would not be possible without the cunning disguise and planning that precedes it). The *Odyssey* presents more generally the means of achievement in a post-heroic world, and in a world where the heroic *kleos* of the Iliadic tradition is crystallized and fixed.

Metis has the power to subdue brawn. Book 23 of the *Iliad* presents the funeral games for Patroclus. As Antilochus, Nestor's son, prepares for a chariot race, Nestor gives sage advice:

It's *metis*, not brawn, that makes the finest woodsman.
By *metis* too that captain holds his ship on course,
Scudding the wine-dark sea though rocked by gales.
By *metis* alone, charioteer outraces charioteer.
(*Il.* 23.359–362, Fagles' translation, slightly modified)

It is by cunning intelligence, intellectual trickery, that man controls nature. It is by *metis* that one triumphs in *agon*. And it is by *metis* that Odysseus outwits and maims Polyphemus. The world of Odysseus lacks the unified purposiveness of war; circumstances are fickle, situations diverse, and Odysseus' supreme resource is his adaptability:

When the individual who is endowed with *metis*, be he god or man, is confronted with a multiple, changing reality whose limitless polymorphic powers render it almost impossible to seize, he can only dominate it— that is to say, enclose it within the limits of a single, unchangeable form within its control—if he proves himself even more multiple, more mobile, more polyvalent than his adversary.[11]

Odysseus is *polytropos*, of many turns. It is this versatility that can free him from any impasse, any knot, that threatens him. He will discover a *poros* to dominate any *aporia*, and his adaptablility will be his greatest resource in a world that lacks the stable identities or simple values.

It is this quality of *metis*, exemplified in the Cyclops episode, that distinguishes Odysseus from Achilles, and even allows him to overcome the dilemma of Achilles. The *kleos*, the honor, of the Iliadic warrior is constituted by those who sing it or witness it. Honor in itself is empty; it must be seen, compensated, or sung to be meaningful. Agamemnon deprives Achilles of Briseis, the outward token of his honor, and Achilles' sense of self-worth is challenged by the bereavement of the external sign. Achilles does not separate his honor from its signifier. *Metis*, on the other hand, continually effects a disjunction between outward appearance and inward truth. It is by *metis* that Odysseus disguises himself, hides himself, speaks one thing while thinking another. Achilles cannot disjoin his honor from its token; Odysseus actively creates this disjunction to achieve his ends. Achilles would challenge Polyphemus with his spear; Odysseus becomes "nobody," abandons his heroic identity, and escapes death. Achilles could not tolerate being "Nobody."

There is a beautiful pun the underlies this episode in the Greek: *Outis* means "nobody," but an alternate form of *outis* is *me tis*. When Polyphemus tells his fellow Cyclopes that "Nobody has harmed him," they reply: "Well, if *me tis* (no one) has harmed you...." *Metis* has harmed him indeed.

Book X
After escaping the ballistic boulders slung by Polyphemus, Odysseus' next landfall is Aeolia. The isle floats adrift on the sea. The Greek adjective "aiolos" means shifty, changeful, glimmering, and King Aiolos commands the winds. After a brief sojourn, Aiolos sends off Odysseus, containing all adverse winds in a bag. But they are destroyed by their *aphradiesin*, "mindlessness." His mutinous crew open the bag, suspecting stashed gold and silver.

Odysseus did not prevent them because he was asleep: in sight of his fatherland, Odysseus could not resist a drowse. In the *Epic of Gilgamesh*, the hero must stay awake for seven days to achieve immortality, a trial he fails. Wakefulness is an epic test. For Odysseus, hero of *metis*, wakefulness is even more essential: it is his total awareness, his perfect presence, which permits him to achieve his victories.

When the bag is opened, the storm winds blow them violently back to Aeolia. In the storm, Odysseus imagines throwing himself into the sea, but beats back the enticing possibility of death. Touching land, Odysseus begs Aeolus to renew his help; but Aeolus refuses. It is an accursed voyage, hated by the immortals, he says.

Putting to sea again, they come next to the Laestrygonians. Like the Cyclopes, these have no farms or cultivated land. A few of Odysseus' men follow a young princess up to the palace of her father, Antiphates. On arrival some are consumed; the rest flea, pursued by savage, boulder-slinging Laestrygones, back to the ships. Odysseus quickly puts to sea again, bewailing those left behind to the cannibal feast.

Next they come to Aeaea, where the goddess Circe dwells. They lie on the beach for two days and nights, "eating their spirit in sorrowing," which is no nourishment for the belly. Odysseus goes to survey the island, and sees smoke rising from a wood hut. He debates in his heart whether to approach the hut right then, but prudently decides to return to his men. On his way he haps upon an antlered buck, which he shoots down.

Circe is the daughter of the sun, and her island is the seat of dawn's rising (12.3). Aeaea (as well as Ogygia and the home of the Cyclopes) offers crops without toil of agriculture. Yet for all its abundance, the very permanence and ease of this life give it a death-like stillness. When Odysseus unloads the buck from his shoulders, and offers it to his men, "till the setting of the sun they sit feasting on the abundant meat and sweet wine." (10.184) The word usually translated as "abundant" is *aspeta*, whose literal meaning is "unspeakable" or "unverbal." It is etymologically related to *epos*—the genre of the *Odyssey*—and the verbs *ennepe* and *espete*, both of which refer to the divinely inspired speech of epic. *Krea aspeta* is "abundant meat," but also rather meat that by its abundance refuses to be the theme of epic song. The paradise situations that Odysseus haps upon in his wanderings are conceived as obstacles because they obviate the heroic achievement that song commemorates.

After they have had their fill of venison, Odysseus speaks:

> O friends! We do not know where is the gloom or the
> dawn,
> Nor where the sun that offers light to mortals sinks
> beneath the earth,
> Nor where it rises: But let's consider quick
> Whether there is still left to us any *metis*. (190–193)

Odysseus is disoriented upon the sea, lost and adrift. But he opposes this disorientation by his *metis*. He is moored and directed by his mind.

He splits his men into two bands, and sends one to investigate Circe's home. The band are falsely reassured when they see Circe weaving and singing, surrounded by tame beasts. Eurylochus, however, sniffed some snare and stayed back. For the rest Circe lays out a meal, but mixes her evil drugs (*kaka pharmaka*) into the food. The effect of the drugs is that the men "utterly forget" their native land. The drugs attack the mind first, and transform them bodily afterwards. Just as the Lotus plant, the threat to their *nostos* is cognitive: amnesia will stay their homeward push. Circe's drug transforms them mentally first, then bodily. Deprived of their memory, the men become pigs. The pig is the lot of the amnesiac.

Eurylochus scampers back to Odysseus to tell him; Odysseus slings his sword over his shoulder and moves to save his men. Hermes intercepts Odysseus to offer him help: he supplies him with the *molu* plant, an antidotal charm to defeat Circe's bitter drugs. Hermes is a liminal god, a god of transitions. He is the *psychopompos*: he ushers souls into the underworld. Odysseus' purpose is also liminal: he is questing to retrieve his men from enchantment, to free their entrapped souls. There is something shamanistic about his role in this episode.

Hermes' herbal potion successfully combats Circe's drugs, and she recognizes the man prophesied long before, Odysseus.

Odysseus insists that she unbind his men before he partakes in the pleasures of love or food, and she complies. Odysseus sojourns there a year in hedonism, before his men tell him to "remember" his *nostos*. He informs Circe that he intends to go, but she tells him that he must visit the underworld to consult the prophet Teiresias. This *nekyia* is the subject of the next book.

Book XI
Odysseus and his crew sail toward the gloom; the sun sets as they glide toward the Western eschaton. They perform the sacrifices and rituals as Circe had instructed, summoning the shades with wine, milk, and blood. Odysseus draws his sword to prevent the thirsty phantoms from tasting the blood before Teiresias.

The first shade to appear is Elpenor ("Hopeman"). Elpenor had lain apart from his companions on the roof of Circe's home, heavy with wine. In the morning, he fell off the roof and broke his neck. Now, in Hades, he implores Odysseus to return to Circe's isle and give him a proper burial. He requests that they heap up a tomb, and plant an oar atop his burial mound. The Homeric word for tomb is *sema*, whose basic meaning is "sign" or "token." The tomb signifies the achievements of living man.

The blind Theban prophet Teiresias comes next, whom Odysseus questions about his "honey-sweet *nostos*." Teiresias warns Odysseus to leave unharmed the cattle of the sun, who graze on Thrinacia, or his hardships in returning will multiply. After he has avenged the suitors, Teiresias continues, Odysseus must go inland on foot with an oar. He must carry the oar so far inland that the people eat their food unmixed with salt, and that someone mistakes the oar for a winnowing fan. Then he must plant the oar in the ground, and propitiate Poseidon with rams and bulls. Even after the satisfaction of his *nostos*, Odysseus is forced to flee home, to flee the center, to become a centrifugal hero. He is bound to continuing exile to appease Poseidon.

As in the encounter with Elpenor, the erect oar again functions as a *sema*. The oar carried and implanted inland is a monument to the weariness of rowing, to the wisdom of the sea. A possible etymology of the name Teiresias is "the weariness of rowing," an etymology found in Homer: "TEIReto d' andron thymos hyp' EIRESIES. [The spirit of the men wearied beneath the rowing.]"[12] We commented above that the crossing from the womb-like comforts of Ogygia to the violent sea allows Odysseus his heroic realization. Where there is no hardship, where the meat is limitless in its abundance, where one need not toil at the oar for his conveyance, the hero's self dissolves. The trial that Tiresias inflicts upon Odysseus is the fitting consummation of his epic voyage: to import the wisdom of the sea, the pain of birth, to the innermost stronghold of land. This is the *sema*'s significance.

Then Odysseus meets his mother, Anticleia. She tells him the situation on Ithaca: Penelope is faithful, Telemachus is alive, but the reckless band of suitors consumes his livelihood. She died of loneliness for her absent son. Three times Odysseus attempts to embrace his dead mother; three times her insubstantial phantom passes untouched through his arms.

After his mother recedes, Odysseus sees and questions a long train of famous women. Odysseus lists them all in his narrative; he becomes a catalogic poet, like Book II of the *Iliad* or sections of Hesiod. The typical poetic catalogue begins with an invocation of the Muse to compensate for the insufficiency of human memory. The catalogue of ships in the *Iliad* begins with an appeal to Muses with perfect knowledge, since men have only the *kleos*, "hearsay." The poet speaks from a stance of distance, of absence, from the described event. Odysseus blurs the distinction between hero and poet: he gives a direct experience and knowledge of the heroines. He is a poet with presence, and as the Muse is a substitute for presence, he does not need her.

After the catalogue, Odysseus breaks his narration, and proposes to the enchanted Phaeacians that all retire to bed. Alcinous insists that he continue, and comments on his narrative abilities: "We do not suppose that you are a dissembler or a braggart ... there is a shape to your words, and you have a good mind. You have spoken a tale knowingly, like a poet." (11.363–368) Odysseus repeatedly fabricates lies to achieve his ends. Athena, in Book XIII, praises him as a consummate dissembler. Yet Alcinous denies that Odysseus is a cunning liar because his words have a certain "shape" (*morphe*). However, it is this very ability to speak with *morphe* that makes Odysseus successful as a liar. How can we evaluate the truth of the tales that Odysseus tells? Some episodes in his wanderings are corroborated at other moments in the *Odyssey*, yet the possibility of falsehoods remains. It would be vain to claim that the whole of Odysseus' narration is artful lie; however, the *Odyssey* has "narrative techniques" that at least "make possible such an evaluation."[13]

Alcinous asks Odysseus if he met any of his old martial comrades from Troy in Hades. He saw several, Odysseus rejoins, the first of them being Agamemnon. Agamemnon tells Odysseus of his own inglorious death, slain like an ox at the crib by Aegisthus. Agamemnon, just like Odysseus, returns home to a perverted feast; he becomes the profane meat. Agamemnon then fumes a fierce diatribe against woman, who are faithless and deceptive. Woman's guile, he says, caused the carnage of his return and of the Trojan War itself. He cautions Odysseus to return home in disguise, and to test his wife.

Odysseus then encounters the exhausted shade of Achilles. No man, says Odysseus, was more blest by fortune than you. You were honored as a god while alive, and now you rule over the dead. Achilles responds:

> Do not console me about death, brilliant Odysseus. I would rather live on the earth as a slave to another, to a landless man without livelihood, than lord over all the wasted dead. (488–491)

The lowest position on earth would be preferable to a kingship over the expired. Achilles, in the *Iliad*, chooses a short, incandescent life of glory over a long life of anonymity. There are two ways to interpret Achilles' bitter response to Odysseus:

a) Achilles is rejecting the heroic *ethos* of the *Iliad*, where life is a small price to pay for everlasting fame. Achilles, now dead, reconsiders the choice he made, and decides any life is preferable to death, no matter how glorious.

b) The numb terror, the mindless oblivion of death is the necessary background to heroic achievement. There is no beatific afterworld to look forward to longingly; death's gloom is the end. But if death were not so horrible, it would trivialize Achilles' choice, because the price of glory would not as great. "Odysseus' well-intentioned but inept attempt to console has the effect of reducing the fearful cost, and therefore the terrible splendor, of Achilles' decision."[14]

Achilles asks Odysseus for news of his son, Neoptolemos. Odysseus tells a proud Achilles that his son never slinks back, but fights valiantly among the first ranks, and has slain innumerable enemies. Hearing this, Achilles departs over the fields of asphodel, "rejoicing that I said his son was preeminent." Achilles' joy in hearing the prowess of his son indicates that he has not rejected the *kleos* that he died to attain, and that his words to Odysseus do not subvert his choice, but subtly confirm it (b).

Odysseus next comes across the shade of Ajax. He and Odysseus had quarreled on the beach of Troy, and now Odysseus begs Ajax to curb his wrath. Ajax turns and speechlessly walks away. The Alexandrian critic, Longinus, quotes this episode to show that silence may be more sublime than words.

Odysseus then sees the torments of Tityos, Tantalus, and Sisyphus, forerunners of the tortured denizens of Dante's *Inferno*. Finally Odysseus sees Hercules, who tells of his own compelled descent into Hades. The *nekyia*, the mortal visiting the underworld, is an epic *topos* in itself. Hercules and Orpheus are precursors in the Greek tradition, while Aeneas and Dante succeed in later epics. Odysseus' association with Hercules in his *nekyia* invites him into the number of heroes.

Book XII

The ships sail back to Aeaea. Odysseus finds the body of Elpenor, and burns his corpse and equipment. They heap up his *sema*, fixing an oar atop the mound. Circe finds them, and all feast on "unspeakable meat" and honeyed wine.

Circe and Odysseus lie alone together, while Odysseus tells of his subterranean wanderings "fittingly" or "in due order" (*kata moiran*). Circe alerts Odysseus to the obstacles that threaten the next leg of his voyage: First he will encounter the Sirens, whose honey-sweet singing seduces men to their own withering.

> ... There are bones
> Of dead men rotting in a pile beside them
> And flayed skins shrivel around the spot. (54–56)

The grassy isle of the Sirens is the inversion of the mythical meadow that is a common *topos* for erotic happenings in Greek poetry. Instead of ever-renewing growth, freshness, and youth, they are surrounded by putrefaction and death. The decomposition of bodies opposes itself to the nature of their song. What they will claim to offer Odysseus is a knowledge unviolated by the entropic motions of the world. The metaphoric expression of the immortality of song in Homer is *kleos aphthiton*, from the root *phthi-*, which is often applied to plants and wildlife in Homer. *Aphthiton*, then, means imperishable or unwilting; it is partially a vegetal metaphor. This scene of rot and decomposition contradicts the nature of song.

Circe then warns Odysseus of Scylla, a fearsome, many-headed monster, and Charybdis, who suck down black water, drawing men to a watery death. None has escaped the vortex of Charybdis but the Argo, "a care to all" (*pasi melousa*). The story of Jason and the Argonauts is a variant, rival epic tradition, which the *Odyssey* here tries agonistically to outdo, by Odysseus' own escape from Charybdis. Odysseus had begun his narration by claiming *he* was "a care to all" (*pasi... melo*).

Odysseus tells the crew what he has heard from Circe—with some cunning omissions. He does not forewarn that six men will be devoured raw by a savage beast. Presumably the great tactician thought it might interfere with their morale.

Odysseus and his crew set off. As they approach the island of the Sirens, Odysseus seals off the ears of all his crew with wax, and commands them to bind him tight to the mast. He alone hears their song.

The two songstresses offer their *terpsis* (joy, delight) and a greater wisdom. Odysseus violently struggles to loose his fetters, but his men bind him tighter. The Sirens beckon Odysseus to return to his Iliadic persona, and to forsake his *nostos*. But they thus beckon him to a world which is closed, immutable, and dead. Their song, which they advertise as perfect, is in fact the skeleton of epic, unfleshed, like the decomposing corpses in their audience.

The classicist Pietro Pucci, who is particularly interested in "intertextual" echoes between the *Iliad* and the *Odyssey*, has shown that the diction of the Sirens unmistakably reproduces the diction of the *Iliad*. The passage is replete with phrases that are unique in the *Odyssey* but occur several times in the other epic.[15]

The Sirens allure Odysseus toward a former self, and so evoke a certain nostalgia. The concept of nostalgia is vital to the *Odyssey*. The word is built from *nostos*, return, and *algos*, suffering, so nostalgia is the suffering caused by the unfulfilled desire to return. His home, on Ithaca, is the endpoint of his voyaging, the goal that animates his epic strivings. The Sirens try to relocate the end of his *nostos* to Troy, the total inversion of his journey. This threatens the complete unraveling of his character.

The Sirens invite Odysseus to switch poems. They seduce him with the past, and toward old, Trojan War paradigms of *kleos*, which have proved insufficient to the challenges of the post-heroic world of Odysseus' wanderings. Pucci claims that the song of the Sirens refers to the "text" of the *Iliad*. Since our knowledge of how two poems of Homer interrelate, and what form they might have taken, is so fragmentary, we must take Pucci's use of "text" as metaphorical. A text is fixed, closed off, and unchanging. The Sirens beckon Odysseus to a past which has become a text, and thus to his own death.

Charles Segal describes the past that the Sirens present as "something frozen and crystallized into lifeless, static form, something dead and past," and thus the heroism is "purely retrospective."[16] The total defeat of the Sirens is the moment that Odysseus strings the bow "like a musician" in Book XXII: then song is not something past and dead. Odysseus transmutes into his own living song.

Because it presents the past as something closed and dead, the song of the Sirens is the perversion of epic: "The Sirens have the *terpsis* of the epic bard, but no contact with the kleos that conquers death."[17] *Kleos* demands to be relived to be meaningful. The verb of hearing, Segal points out, consistently used to describe the apprehension of the Sirens' song, is *akouein*, and not *kluein*. *Kluein* is etymologically related to *kleos*, and so the repetition of *akouein* emphasizes the literal, physical nature of the hearing, and its distance from the vital hearing of epic. Their song can be blocked by sealing the physical organ of hearing since it is but the ghostly shadow of epic. Further, the "Sirens speak the language of 'knowing' ... but no word of 'memory' or 'remembering' characterizes their song."[18] Memory is the true source of heroic song, not the sterile recitation or information retrieval of pure knowing. The bard recreates, resuscitates, and recalls to mind the past; memory breathes and quickens.

Sailing beyond the Sirens, Odysseus' ships enter the strait between Scylla and Charybdis. Disregarding the advice of Circe, Odysseus dons his "glorious armor" (*kluta teukhea*) and brandishes two spears to face the dread beast. Scylla, unseen by Odysseus, snatches up six of his men and eats them alive. Odysseus, motionless in his armor, displays the pathetic impotence of Iliadic modes of heroism in the face of new challenges of the sea.

Though Odysseus insists that the crew sail past Thrinacia without mooring, Eurylochus convinces him to let them harbor. After they disembark, the south wind blows unceasingly for a month, and they are becalmed without food. Odysseus wanders off to pray, but falls asleep. Eurylochus rouses the crew to mutiny, and they slay several of Helios' cattle for food. The

Sun threatens Zeus that, if he does not punish their insolence, he will shine among the dead, and invert the cosmos. As the men roast meat on the spits, there are portents of ill: the hides crawl on the ground, the meat bellows as it cooks. When they put to the open sea again, Zeus wracks their ship in a fierce storm. Odysseus, drifting on flotsam, is almost swallowed by Charybdis, but he holds desperately onto a fig tree to stay above water. He escapes. Here ends his tale to the enchanted Phaeacians.

The prologue of the *Odyssey* mentions the slaughter of the sun's cattle as the act of overweening insolence for which Odysseus' crew was robbed of its *nostos*. What does this act of insolence signify? There are 350 sheep and 350 cattle grazing on Thrinacia, and their number neither multiplies nor diminishes (*pthinousi*). Aristotle states directly that the livestock of the sun represent the days and nights of the year. The cattle assume a cosmic symbolic import: they are markers of the normal passage of time. When the crew kill the cattle, they are not merely offending Helios. They are desecrating time.[19]

Calypso offered Odysseus timelessness, a life of light immortality with a goddess, but he chose death and *nostos*. His love, his achievement, his meaning, his heroism all depend upon his death. He could not love with the same urgency, sail home with the same determination, or war with the same sense of tragedy if human life were not so ephemeral. Immortality would trivialize his past achievement, and also his nostalgia. Timelessness—on both Ogygia and Thrinacia—is a besetting trial, because the absence of time dissolves human identity. "In its first stages, the temporal horizon is simply a manifestation of memory."[20] Memory is the mind's representation of time. The dissolution of time destroys memory, and forgetfulness obscures our sense of time. The slaughter of the cattle violates time; as memory is the internalization of time, temporal disorientation is a type of amnesia. Many of the trials in Odysseus' fantastical wanderings are couched in cognitive language: The lotus flower, the song of the Sirens, and the magic of Circe all threaten "forgetfulness of *nostos*." The *nostos* is a return to the past, to a region of memory, and so the deepest threat to its completion is amnesia.

Book XIII

Odysseus' yarn is complete; the banqueters sit in silence, spellbound. Alcinous pierces the quiet with a promise of lavish guest-gifts, and urges all Phaeacians to give abundantly. Preparations are made for Odysseus' conveyance, and all enjoy a final feast together. Odysseus cannot lightly enjoy the pleasures of food and wine; he keeps impatiently turning his head to the sun, eager to see it set. When the world darkens he will at last move homeward.

Odysseus "crosses the threshold" (13.63). There is a clear symbolism in the threshold: this is the moment of crossing, the passage back to home. The threshold is no longer blocked; there is no Polyphemus to close the mouth of the cave. When Odysseus settles into the ship, soon sleep falls on his eyelids: "unawakening, most sweet, most like death." At the great moment of transition, from homing wanderer to homecoming, Odysseus is subdued by a deathlike slumber. The deep sleep is a symbolic death at the moment of unconscious liminality, the return.

The Phaeacians unload Odysseus on his native shore, while he continues to drowse. Poseidon is upset that Odysseus has returned, despite his intention to impose ongoing hardship, and that the Phaeacians so artfully and automatically master the sea. Poseidon turns to stone the ship that had carried Odysseus homeward, while Phaeacians look on, bewildered and petrified. Alcinous recognizes a divine prophecy of old—Poseidon will smite a ship, and hem them in with mountains to block them from the sea.

Odysseus awakes, and despairs: he does not recognize where he is. When he first opens his eyes to his native land, the "life-giving earth" of his fathers, everything is foreign, as if he were on the other side of the world. All things seem to have other shapes (*alloeidea*, 194). He bemoans his endless exile.

Athena appears in the guise of a shepherd boy. She reveals to Odysseus that this strange land is indeed his home. He rejoices inwardly, though remains cautious, detached. In response, he weaves an elaborate lie of his history—the first of the so-called "Cretan tales." He will tell versions of this lie to Eumaeus in Book XIV, the suitors in XVII, and Penelope in XIX. The permutations of this tale are a series of subtle manipulations, of disguised revelations, and murky mixtures of falsehood and truth. In this instance, he pretends to be an anonymous man from Crete, who has killed Orsilochus, son of Idomeneus, for attempting to steal his Trojan booty. He bribed the Phoenicians to give him passage to Pylos or Elis, but they were blown off course by storm gales. The Phoenicians dropped him off here.

Athena, of course, quickly perceives the trickery, but is delighted at his cunning and ability to dissemble. "One would have to be cunning and stealthy (*epiklopos*) to surpass you in all wiles" (291–292). She praises him for his "variegated *metis*" (*poikilometa*, 293), his supreme adaptability (polytropy) that is his greatest strength. And, in fact, Athena counsels him to use his cunning, to remain in disguise, to avenge the suitors. She, with a tap of her wand, makes him "unrecognizable" (*agnoston*). He alone possesses the knowledge that the king has returned to exact vengeance. Athena, granting him the power of disguise, has also granted him the power of knowledge: he will use this power to control the recognitions that are the main motif of the second half of the *Odyssey*. Secret knowledge—or rather knowledge shared only by character and poet—immediately makes possible the ironies and half-truths that dominate this portion of the poem.

Even after Athena assures Odysseus that he has arrived home, he doggedly refuses to believe. "I do not believe that I have come to clear Ithaca; I have wandered to some other land" (324–326). The material tokens, the mere appearance of Ithaca, do not reveal to him that he is home. Then Athena shows him the old harbor, and the "long-leafed olive tree" he knew 20 years prior. The mist clears from his eyes, and he kisses the earth in joy. Athena has located Ithaca not on a map of the sea, but in the map of his memory. The physical return to Ithaca is nothing; he weeps as if he were still marooned on Calypso's isle. It is the return to a place of memory, a familiar place, that constitutes his homecoming.

Recognition is the basic mental act of the second half of the *Odyssey*, whereby Odysseus completes his return. The *nostos* is both a journey toward Ithaca, and a journey toward a place of memory. That journey is not complete without the mental re-appropriation of the fatherland, denoted by the Greek word *anagnorisis*, recognition. Aristotle says of the second half of the *Odyssey*, it is "recognitions throughout" (*anagnorisis diolou*).[21] Recognition is the process whereby knowledge is mapped onto reality, and memory is relocated in the world of appearance.

Athena suggests that Odysseus stay on Ithaca in disguise while she goes to Sparta to summon Telemachus. She sent Telemachus to Sparta, she explains, to search for news (*kleos*) of Odysseus. The Greek word *kleos*, much like the Latin *fama*, means "fame, renown," and also "report, rumor, news." Telemachus has gone in search of his father's *kleos* in order to gain some for himself. Odysseus asks, "Why did you not just tell him? Was it in order that he too might, perhaps, wander and suffer hardships upon the unwearying sea, while others consume his livelihood?" (418–419). Odysseus' question implies that Athena deliberately put Telemachus in a place analogous to his own. Just like his father, Telemachus will suffer at sea, while his home is profanely eaten away. Athena sent him so that he might, also like his father, win "good *kleos*" among men (422).

Athena touches Odysseus with her wand, shrivels the skin around his bones, darkens his eyes, and wraps around him a tattered garment so that he is unrecognizable. She places in his hand a *skeptron*—a word that means both a king's staff and a beggar's walking stick.

Book XIV

Odysseus hikes up from the cove to the hut of the Eumaeus, the "noble swineherd," "who cared for Odysseus' possessions more than any other servant" (3–4). Odysseus comes upon the pens built by Eumaeus' industry, wherein Odysseus' livestock are hemmed. As Odysseus approaches, watchdogs bark violently, announcing to Eumaeus the presence of a stranger. Eumaeus' first words express grief for his absent master, which characterizes him as loyal to Odysseus, even through years of distance. To be disguised allows Odysseus to discern true loyalties in his house. Eumaeus warmly invites the stranger in, explaining that "all strangers and beggars are from Zeus" (13.57–58). This hospitality distinguishes Eumaeus from the less welcoming hosts that Odysseus has encountered in his wandering, and aligns him with the morally right in the *Odyssey*'s moral world.

Eumaeus offers his guest a meal. He roasts a baby pig—the fatted hogs, he adds, are being consumed by the insolent suitors. Odysseus property was *aspetos*—literally, "unspeakable," too large to tell. We encountered this word in the narrative of Odysseus' wanderings to describe the paradises that Odysseus comes to: the food is *aspeta*, unspeakably abundant, on Circe's isle, and on Thrinicia. The suitors feast on Ithaca as if they were in paradise. Food is an important area of life where transgression can occur. The pig farm of Eumaeus is symbolically linked to the cattle of the sun: in the perverted feast, the suitors transgress in cosmic ways, by their own insolence and ignorance.[22]

After Odysseus has satisfied his craving for food and wine, he asks Eumaeus who his master was, who lorded over so much. Odysseus suggests that, since he has wandered far, he may even know some news of him. Eumaeus discredits him: wanderers, in need of sustenance, tell lies. This passage opens up a series of puns and wordplays that indicate an ironic connection between wandering and truth. The Greek word for wanderer is *aletes*, and the word for truth is *alethes*. In Homer's time, the difference between "t" and "th" was that the latter was aspirated, so that the two forms are even more homophonic.

Odysseus tells Eumaeus that he has "wandered far" (*alethen*, the past tense of *alaomai*, to wander). Eumaeus responds that "wanderers lie [*aletai pseudont'*] and never wish to speak truth [*alethea*]" (13.124–125). Wandering is both the means of acquiring and disseminating the truth, and the situation that compels men to lie. Odysseus is, according to Charles Segal, "a master of lies and disguise who, like his poet, achieves his ultimate truth through devious paths and through a paradoxical mixture of truth and false appearances."[23] He is also a man who, ironically, achieves his *kleos*, and creates an identity for himself, due to his ability to disguise and dissemble. The punning on wandering and truth articulates this irony.

After Eumaeus dismisses the guileful news of beggars, he names his master: "It is longing for Odysseus that so distresses me" (14.144). Just as in the proem of the poem, the actual utterance of Odysseus' name is delayed, suppressed. "I am ashamed to say his name, though he is absent," Eumaeus continues. The name "Odysseus," from the verb *odyssomai*, could be translated as "Man of Pain" or "Trouble" (both of these translations preserve the transitive symmetry of his name: he is both sufferer of pain and dispenser of pain). Names, in the *Odyssey*, are more than just arbitrary signifiers. They are performative and descriptive, relics of the primitive tendency to believe in the magic power of the proper noun. The story of Odysseus' naming will be considered in Book XIX, but the encounter with Polyphemus signifies just this superstition: it is the utterance of the proper name, in boast, that incurs the curse, and makes possible the wrath of Poseidon.

Odysseus assures Eumaeus his intent is not to deceive, and swears a solemn oath that Odysseus shall return. He explains: "That man is hateful to me like the gates of death, who, yielding to poverty, babbles deceitfully." This is a clear echo of Achilles famous speech to Odysseus in Book IX of the *Iliad*: "That man is hateful to me like the gates of death, who says one thing but hides another in his heart." In the mouth of Achilles, these words voice contempt for Odysseus as rhetorician, a man who achieves his victories by cunning speech and not strength, by creating disjunction between the inside and the outside. Odysseus ironically mouths his disdain for lies in Achilles' own words, just before an elaborate false history. As Jean Starobinski writes, "He [Odysseus] lies and speaks the truth at once, lying in order to make a heartfelt truth erupt, to find out if kith and kin have kept faith with him."24 Odysseus lies to discover the truth, not "yielding to poverty."

Odysseus answers Eumaeus' questions about his birth with the second "Cretan tale," the second in a series of fabricated histories with which Odysseus disguises himself on Ithaca. He claims he was born of Hylax, on Crete. He was a warrior, "no coward in battle," who fought for nine years at Troy. After Troy he made a profiteering and piratical excursion to Egypt. There, the "insolence" (*hubris*) of his crew rouses the Egyptians to attack them, and they are destroyed. He begs in supplication to the Egyptian king, who pities him and takes him in. He stays in Egypt for seven years. Then a deceitful Phoenician beguiles him into boarding a ship with the object of selling him to slavery. Zeus destroys the ship with a thunderbolt, and the nameless Cretan drifts to the Thesprotians, who had entertained Odysseus. It was from the Thesprotians, the nameless beggar tells Eumaeus, that he learned that Odysseus was alive and had consulted an oracle at Dodona about whether to come home openly or in secret. This second Cretan Tale exhibits elements of the true tale of Odysseus: the timeframe is identical, he warred at Troy, sojourned somewhere seven years, somewhere else one year, and was destroyed by the *hubris* of his crew. Truth and falsehood blend indistinctly.

Eumaeus professes not to believe that Odysseus could be near. He tells of an Aetolian who lied to Penelope that Odysseus would soon approach, just to procure a meal. Odysseus again swears a mighty oath, telling Eumaeus that he can toss him off a cliff if his prophesy does not materialize. The two sit for supper. This time Eumaeus slaughters (with appropriate sacrificial oblation) an old, fatted boar. The progression from baby pig to mature boar indicates some growth in trust and friendship between the swineherd and the king.

The cautiously deceitful Odysseus then fabricates a tale about Troy. He tells Eumaeus that he (the Cretan), Odysseus, and Menelaus had led a clandestine ambush on Troy. They camped in the brushwood around the city for the frosty night.

The Cretan, however, had forgotten his cloak, and was dying of cold. (The fictional) Odysseus devises a ruse whereby one of the ambushers is sent back to the ships, and the Cretan slips into his cloak. In response to the story, Eumaeus gives the stranger a cloak to keep him warm for the night.

The fictional story of the disguised Odysseus is totally un-Iliadic. No hero would complain of being cold in the Iliad. Achilles, the exemplary Iliadic hero, rejects food in Book XIX, because he is so eager to fight. The heroes, in their sublimity, never feel cold or hot, or any other intrusion of the body (besides, perhaps, death). In Odysseus' story, a (supposed) hero complains of being cold and needing a blanket. This is a parody of the Trojan War, a moment of mock-epic.

Previously, Eumaeus told the stranger: "Readily would you too, old man, fashion a story, if one would give you a cloak and a tunic to wear" (Loeb 131–132). Here Odysseus has done just that: fashioned a story to acquire a cloak. "You have not spoken without profit," Eumaeus tells him. *Kerdos* (gain, profit) is semantically linked to cleverness (*metis*) and deceit.[25] It appears, then, that Odysseus has become the beggar who lies for his sustenance that Eumaeus fears. At the same time, Odysseus has obliquely confirmed the truth of his story, which was intended to give a picture of the cunning intelligence, the wiliness, the *kerdosune*, of Odysseus. All these layers of ambiguous truth and falsehood operate in his tale.

Eumaeus retires to sleep among the boars, and Odysseus inwardly rejoices that his servant so diligently cares for his property.

Book XV

Athena visits a sleepless Telemachus in Sparta. She urges him to hasten home before the suitors devour all, and warns that Penelope's father and kinsmen are pressuring her to marry. Is the threat that Penelope might relent real? Or is Athena just spurring Telemachus to action? An alternative mythical version of the *Odyssey* in antiquity told that Penelope slept with the suitors and had illegitimate children, and many critics believe that elements of this alternate myth rise to the surface at various points of the canonical *Odyssey*, introducing doubt into Penelope's perfect faithfulness.

Telemachus rises and asks Menelaus to send him off, who insists that Telemachus accept guest-gifts and a final meal. Helen gives to Telemachus a finely embroidered robe, her own handiwork. She say its will be a *mnema*—a monument or memento—for Telemachus' future wife to wear. Telemachus' future wife, in wearing it, will herself become a *mnema* to Helen—an ominous portent, since Helen's failures as a wife are so prominent. In addition, even the discussion of Telemachus' marriage signals his growing maturity. During the first few books in Ithaca, the suggestion of marriage would have seemed incongruous, as he seemed only a boy.

As Menelaus and Telemachus exchange farewells, a mountain eagle soars by with a goose in its claws. Helen offers her mantic interpretation of the bird-sign: Odysseus "will soon come down in fury on his house" (Fitz. 218).

Telemachus and Peisistratus land on Pylos. Telemachus insists that he must leave Peisistratus and launch again that moment, lest the garrulous old Nestor detain him and keep him from pressing business. Before pushing off, Telemachus meets Theoclymenus, a seer and prophet. Homer introduces his story in a digression on his parentage, and then Theoclymenus explains to Telemachus that he has fled home after he murdered a cousin. Telemachus welcomes him and offers food and passage. Athena's favoring wind propels the ship toward Ithaca.

The narrative shifts to Odysseus in the tent of Eumaeus. Odysseus suggests that he leave, and unburden the swineherd. Eumaeus kindly rebukes him, assuring him he is no burden. Odysseus thanks him and adds: "There is nothing more evil for mortals than roving: for the sake of a destructive belly [*gaster*] men suffer woes" (344–345). Here the "belly"—a prominent organ for Odysseus—becomes the impetus for wandering. It is an emblem of human unfulfilment, and an engine of motion.

Odysseus asks Eumaeus of his own parents and biography. Eumaeus happily agrees to relate: "These autumn nights are long | ample for story-telling and for sleep|... in later days a man | can find a charm in old adversity" (Fitz. 478–488). After this prelude on pleasures of stories Eumaeus tells of his own pitiful life: he was a wealthy boy who was guilefully kidnapped by a slave woman who was herself seduced by a Phoenician. Finally "the wind and the water" conveyed him to Ithaca, where he was purchased by Laertes. Eumaeus tells the story straightforwardly, never indulging any maudlin excess. Odysseus sympathizes deeply: he too knows the unique pain of being exiled and compelled by the capricious "wind and water."

Charles Segal calls the wind and the water "the material embodiments of the chance forces of life," and interprets the stories exchanged in the swineherd's hut as follows:

> The life stories of the two men illustrate the chance incidents of life, the power of fortune (*tuche*) in this unstable world of ships and sailors, the precariousness of identity and status once one leaves the security of one's *oikos* (house)...[26]

Kingship, wealth, and authority require the stable structures of the household and town: amid the lawless Cyclopes, such distinctions are meaningless. The world of the *Iliad* was structured simply and discernibly; the world of the *Odyssey* is less sure. Odysseus himself has had to undergo transformative inversions to survive outside the borders of humanly imposed order.

The focus briefly returns to Telemachus. As the two major strands of the narrative—the journey and growth of Telemachus, and the return of Odysseus—come closer to each other, the narration alternates more rapidly between them. In narrative theory this is called the "interlace technique"—the story jumps between the threads more quickly before the threads finally intertwine.

Telemachus lands on Ithaca. Another bird-sign is interpreted by Theoclymenus to signify that Odysseus' bloodline will remain in power. Telemachus straps on his sandals and hikes toward the small hut where Eumaeus and his father exchange their stories.

Book XVI

As Telemachus approaches the hut of Eumaeus, the guard dogs fawn innocuously. Odysseus interprets this to mean the visitor is familiar and friendly; he soon learns it is his son. Telemachus and Eumaeus greet each other warmly, and Eumaeus' interior is described in a notable simile:

> Think of a man whose dear and only son,
> born to him in exile, reared with labor,
> has lived ten years abroad and now returns:
> how would that man embrace his son! Just so
> the herdsman clapped his arms around Telemachus ...
> (Fitz. 23–27)

This is the first of the so-called "reverse similes": the metaphor employed to expose the emotion of one character as the actual emotional experience of another. Here, Odysseus *is* a father returned from exile to see his only son; Eumaeus is *like* a father returned from exile. Homer will use several more of these "reverse similes." They serve to emphasize the emotional consonance in Odysseus' home and allies, and hint at their oneness of purpose and of mind.

Telemachus then calls Eumaeus *atta*, a remnant of baby-talk, roughly equivalent to "daddy." This further confirms their closeness. He asks Eumaeus to go inform his mother of his safe arrival. Athena likens herself to a woman and visits them, though she is invisible to all except Odysseus and the dogs. The Greek verb here used for sight is *noese*, whose meaning exceeds simple vision and denotes a kind of peering through appearances. *Noesis* is the word Plato uses for "intellection," the privileged vision of the ideal forms.

After Eumaeus departs, Athena glorifies Odysseus with youth and fresh beauty. To an awed Telemachus, the man appears to be a god. Odysseus replies:

> No god. Why take me for a god? No, no.
> I am that father whom your boyhood lacked
> and suffered pain for lack of. I am he. (Fitz. 220–223)

The first word of Odysseus' revelation to Telemachus is *ou tis*: precisely the name he assumed to deceive the Cyclopes. Here *ou tis* means "not a," but the echo of his previously adopted name is unmistakable: at the very moment of self-revelation to his son, he echoes his self-concealment to the Cyclops. There is another pun in the Greek: In the same metrical slot of the first and second lines of this response are the phrases *theos eimi* and *teos eimi* ("a god I am [not]" and "your [father] I am"). The barely perceptible difference between the aspirated and unaspirated "t" separates Odysseus from divinity. To Telemachus (who in a fatherless boyhood might have imagined his father as something of a god), this pun might heighten the numinous aura attending this stranger/father. Telemachus is at first incredulous, but he finally believes. Father and son embrace, weeping.

This episode is the first in a series of recognitions by members of his household that will reintegrate Odysseus to his former roles: father, husband, king. As Simon Goldhill puts it:

That this is the first act of mutual recognition is important not merely for the workings of revenge— Odysseus needs Telemachus' support—but also for the thematic stress on the relations between father and son in the patriarchal and patrilineal *oikos*.... To return to the fatherland is to return to the role of the father.[27]

It is precisely this patrilineal structure of the *oikos* (household) that is directly threatened by the suitors: they could usurp the kingship, Telemachus' property, and his mother, and subvert the male line that traces through Odysseus.

Goldhill then points out an important difference between this recognition scene and later ones: there is no *sema*, no sign to incite recognition or confirm identity. "Recognition is part of the relationship to be recognized." That is, fatherhood is not verifiable or self-evident like motherhood. Telemachus says in Book I, "no one really knows his own father" (1.216). Since the fatherhood can never be proved (before modern science), it is a role that is defined culturally and defined by authority. "The son needs to accept the father as the father (as a father *recognizes* his children)—the gestures that maintain structured (patriarchal, patrilineal) authority in the *oikos*."[28]

Odysseus and Telemachus together begin planning the eventual *mnesterophonia*—"slaying of the suitors." The suitors meanwhile are exasperated that Telemachus has evaded their ambush. The ferocious Antinous recommends the immediate murder of Telemachus. He is countered by Amphinomus—whom Homer alone among the suitors calls *euphron*, of sound mind. He counsels restraint, and prevails. Penelope then makes a radiant appearance among them, and fiercely lambastes the malicious Antinous, who is deceitfully and sycophantically defended by Eurymachus.

In the hut, at Eumaeus' returning, Athena transforms Odysseus back into a beggar. They all eat their fill of a young pig—the meats have become choicer as Eumaeus and the disguised Odysseus build trust and solidarity. All three "take the gift of sleep" (481).

Book XVII

At dawn, Telemachus returns to town. Arriving home, Homer tells us, he "steps over the stone threshold" (30). We have already commented how the imagery of the threshold suggests moments of transition and crossing. This is, for Telemachus, a liminal moment: he left home as a boy, a *pais*, and is returning a man (*aner*). The thematic import of the threshold as a separating border—between home and exile, *oikos* and nature—will increase in the later books of the *Odyssey*.

Penelope descends from her high chamber to greet and kiss her son. She is alike, Homer says, to "Atemis or golden Aphrodite" (37). Artemis was the virginal hunter-goddess, whereas Aphrodite is the promiscuous and playful goddess of *eros*. Artemis and Aphrodite represent two poles of female sexual behavior. Side by side, they offer a rather bipolar description, and perhaps suggest the period of sexual confusion that Penelope is about to enter, provoked by the newly arrived stranger.

Before they can discuss his journey, Telemachus goes into town to retrieve Theoclymenus, the seer that embarked in Pylos. Coming back home, he feigns ignorance about the whereabouts of his father, though quotes Menelaus' simile of he lion verbatim: Odysseus will return to his hall and bed like a lion upon a doe and her sucklings. Odysseus was also compared to a lion in Book VI, before meeting the princess Nausikaa (6.130). There he is like a lion whose *gaster* (belly) goads him to hunt: a lion's *gaster* demands to be filled by flesh. The lion, however, is a heroic animal, and so is not impelled solely by *gaster*. Lion similes are frequent in the *Iliad*, where the lion often has a *thumos*—the untranslatable organ with which Achilles would have felt his rage. The lion is impelled alternately by *thumos* and *gaster*, and the *Odyssey* in many ways replaces Achilles' *thumos* with Odysseus' *gaster* and treats the two organs—the one spiritual and metaphorical, the other physiological—as though synonymous.

As Telemachus finishes, Theoclymenus prophesies that Odysseus is indeed already on the island, ready to "sow evil" for the suitors. The suitors, meanwhile, are lazily gaming outside the house, enjoying (*terponto*) the javelin and discus. Theirs is a life of pure *terpsis*—pleasure—without any serious or meaningful action and hardship. They have, in effect, replicated for themselves the paradise conditions of pleasure and abundance that were offered to Odysseus to stagnate his journey home. But, as we have seen, in the world of Homer one cannot live in these conditions without forfeiting part of one's humanity.

Odysseus and Eumaeus continue on the road to town. Odysseus requests a walking stick to ease his way, and Eumaeus graciously obliges. Immediately afterward, they light upon Melanthius, a particularly arrogant servant of Odysseus. Melanthius taunts the disguised king with insults and kicks him. Odysseus bears the insults patiently, silently, though intent on future revenge. Odysseus' success will depend on his ability to control violent sallies of emotion.

As Odysseus and Eumaeus tarry outside the gate of the palace, Odysseus once again references his belly, his *gaster*: "In no way is it possible to hide an eager and destructive belly, which gives many evils to men" (286–287). The line is an unmistakable reference to the opening of the *Iliad*. I quote in Greek and translate as literally as possible:

Menin...
oulomenen, he muri' Achaiois alge' etheken... (*Il.* 1.1–2)

Rage...
Destructive, which countless pains for the Achaeans made.

Gastera...
oulomenen, he polla kak' anthropoisi diosi

Belly...
Destructive, which many evils to men gives ... (286–287)

Odysseus' belly is syntactically and metrically situated exactly like Achilles' rage. Odysseus' belly is the engine of his heroic action, just as Achilles' rage is the engine of his. Pietro Pucci, in a series of studies on "intertextuality" between the *Iliad* and *Odyssey*, argues that Odysseus' belly is emblematic of his heroism, whereas the *thumos*—the spirit, the drive—is emblematic of Iliadic heroism.[29]

As Odysseus speaks, an old dog lying neglected on a heap of dung tries to lift its ear and wag its tail. This is Argus, whom Odysseus left as a puppy and who now recognizes his master. This short episode with Argus is among the most poignant and memorable of the *Odyssey*. Left as a young puppy, eager and swift, Argus has been neglected in the 20 years of Odysseus' absence, and now lies abused and decrepit. After this brief happiness—which he barely has the strength to realize—at seeing his master after 20 years, he dies. The dog is suggestive of the more general decline and malaise in the house of Odysseus: healthy and vigorous when Odysseus departed, and now abused and sickly. The dog also has close similarities to his master (as many critics have pointed out), and also to Laertes. The dog is also thematically important as another early scene of recognition: as such, it is unusual because it involves neither Odysseus' subtle disguising and revelation by speech, nor any tangible *sema*. The verb used for the dog's sight here is *noesai*— the same verb used in Book XVI to describe Odysseus' vision of Athena (see above). Here, as there, the verb denotes a special type of sight, a seeing through the surface.

Odysseus enters the palace and begs for morsels from the suitors and hosts. Telemachus indulges him with a loaf and some roast meat. Odysseus gives another false autobiography or "Cretan tale" to the assembled diners (for the first, see Book XIII above). But he modifies it slightly: There is no mention of supplicating the king of Egypt, nor of the Thesprotions. Instead Odysseus says that the Egyptians give him to a *xeinos* in Cyprus. Perhaps this subtle modification is meant to emphasize the obligations of *xenia*, guest-friendship, which the suitors are so flagrantly violating.[30]

When Odysseus implores Alcinoos to give some food, the haughty suitor hurls a footstool that bruises Odysseus' arm. Though he and Telemachus are both raging at this insult, they patiently bear it.

Penelope's curiosity is aroused by the new stranger, and she asks Eumaeus to bring him to her for questioning about her lost husband. She utters an impulsive prayer for Odysseus to return and repay these impudent suitors, and as she finishes Telemachus sneezes loudly. Sneezes in antiquity, being inexplicable and involuntary, were thought to be ominous and portentous. Penelope interprets this sneeze positively.

Odysseus agrees to meet her at sundown.

Book XVIII

Irus, a public beggar, enters the *megaron* (great hall). He insolently insults and threatens Odysseus who, with total equanimity, reproves his boasting. When Irus rejoins, with even more outrageous arrogance, Antinous laughs happily: Here, he says, is a serendipitous *terpolen*—object of pleasure or sport. He encourages the jousting by offering a stuffed stomach—*gaster*—to the victor. Odysseus replies that he would prefer not to fight, but his belly—*gaster*—impels him. He asks the suitors not to interfere with the fight, to which Telemachus replies: "Stranger, if your spirit (*thumos*) and bold heart compel you to ward off this man, do not fear any of the other Achaeans" (61-3). Telemachus has changed the motivating energy of Odysseus from *gaster* (belly) to *thumos* (spirit). As we have seen, the *thumos* is the fundamental force behind Iliadic action, whereas the *gaster* often motivates the *Odyssey*. Pietro Pucci writes about this interchange of belly and spirit in this episode:

> These lines serve to mask and unmask Odysseus, confirming and reminding us of the double persona as he plays the beggar.... When Telemachus speaks, only apparently quoting his father, it is to intimate that Odysseus actually fights as an Iliadic hero....[31]

Additionally, in this interplay between belly and spirit one can read the suggestion that even the *Iliad*, for all its sublimity, cannot outrun the facts of the human body. This is a fundamentally Aristophanic stance: denying unadulterated sublimity or spirituality by reminding us of our (often disgusting) physicality.

Odysseus responds to Irus' *braggadocio* by hastily dispatching him with a jaw-shattering blow. The fight with Irus, in many ways, prefigures the ultimate confrontation with the suitors. H. D. F. Kitto discusses it as a "paradigmatic myth":

> Irus is insolent, as are the suitors too; Odysseus quells his insolence, as he will quell theirs; Athena helps him against Irus as she will help them against him....[32]

Kitto explains further how this episode exemplifies divine involvement in the whole of the *Odyssey*: the gods—often with humans as their agents—punish lawlessness.

As Irus lies dazed and beaten outside the palace, Athena visits Penelope and inspires in her a desire to show herself before the suitors, in order to inflame the suitor's desire and display her splendor to Odysseus. Penelope laughs "idly" or "aimlessly" (*akhreion*).[33] She hastily lies to her servant that she desires to go urge her son to avoid the suitors. The very fact that she lies bespeaks some guilt or confusion about her motivations. Athena then—against Penelope's will—puts her to sleep and beautifies her with ambrosia. She awakes and appears before the suitors, and her beauty is so intense that is "looses their knees"—a common Iliadic circumlocution for death in battle. She chides Telemachus for letting the strange guest (the disguised Odysseus) be treated so poorly; she rejects Eurymachus' lusty flattery and recalls her husband's parting instruction to remarry when their son grows a beard. Finally, she tells her disgust with the behavior of the suitors, who constantly consume without giving gifts. The suitors then promise lavish gifts. Odysseus "rejoices" (281) when he hears all of this, because Penelope has charmed the suitors and acquired gifts.

This scene has puzzled many critics, who have tried to disentangle Penelope's motives in showing herself to the suitors and Odysseus' subsequent emotional response, which seems somehow inappropriate. Why should Odysseus rejoice to hear Penelope suggest she will remarry, or to see her mistreatment by the suitors? Even the behavior of Penelope was condemned in antiquity: *Regina prope ad meretrcias artes descendit* (the queen descends almost to the arts of a courtesan).[34] Many have claimed that this scene (or parts of it) is an intrusion of the ubiquitous *Barbeiter*—a later editor or compiler modifying or adding to an authentic Homer—and therefore lacks internal consistency. Other critics have sought to vindicate the appropriateness of the scene. The German critic Uvo Holscher, for example, argues:

Why does doubt not assail him about the faithfulness of his wife? Because she has powerfully expressed her aversion to the new marriage. The "other intentions" she [Penelope] had in mind are not a secret plan, they are the feelings of the heart.[35]

Whatever the complexity and inconsistency of the scene, it is the first moment that Odysseus sees his wife after his long absence. Perhaps his happiness is simply a result of that.

Odysseus offers a group of young serving-women to help tend the fire, but Melantho, an impudent maid and sister of Melanthius, jeers at him. She had disgraced Penelope, Homer tells us, by sleeping with the suitors. Odysseus tersely terrifies the ladies so they disperse.

Eurymachus, then, hurls an unprovoked and gratuitous insult at Odysseus, who calmly denies him. Odysseus must then duck under another ballistic footstool, this time from the hand of Melanthius.

Telemachus exhorts all to return home, having drunk too much. They pour libations and retire.

Book XIX

Odysseus and Telemachus collusively hide all of the arms in the main hall in preparation for the next day's business. To Telemachus' joyful wonder, Athena alights their activities. Their work complete, Odysseus sends Telemachus to bed, while he stays awake to "test" his mother (the Greek word for test is *etherizo*, from the root *eris*, "strife or competition," indicating some confrontational component to the questioning).

Penelope and the disguised Odysseus comfortably recline to converse. When Penelope asks the stranger his name and homeland, Odysseus responds with praise:

> ... Your name
> Has gone out under heaven like the sweet
> honor of some god-fearing king, who rules
> in equity over the strong.... (Fitz. 129–132)

Helen P. Foley has called such similes, where the subject changes gender in metaphor, "reverse similes." Often, as here, the simile could be read as interpreting some characteristic of either Penelope or Odysseus in terms of the other one: Penelope, the renowned queen, is understood metaphorically in terms of Odysseus. According to Foley, the similes do more than simply indicate like-mindedness or emotional kinship between husband and wife. They are symptoms of the *Odyssey's* fundamentally comedic structure of social disruption and restoration. Further, they show the interdependence of the two genders in effecting and maintaining this restoration.[36]

Penelope diverts the beggar's compliments by claiming that her bloom and beauty departed along with her husband 20 years prior. She briefly tells her own story with the arrogant suitors, and her cunning ruse of the shroud. Again, she asks the beggar's ancestry.

Odysseus fabricates another Cretan tale, this time naming himself Aithon. In Greek this name mean "shining" or "flickering" as fire. The pseudonym is quite appropriate: it allies Odysseus with the forces of fire, the most shifty, adaptable, and rapidly changing of the elements. "Aithon" befits our polytropic hero, engaged at this very moment in a feat of deception.

He tells how Odysseus visited him in Crete after being blown off course *en route* to Troy. Odysseus makes his words "so alike to truth" that Penelope weeps. Homer give a particularly beautiful and memorable simile:

> ... The skin
> of her pale face grew moist the way pure snow
> softens and glistens in the mountains, thawed
> by Southwind after powdering from the West,
> and, as snow melts, mountain streams run full:
> so her white cheeks were wetted by these tears
> shed for her lord—and he close by her side.
> (Fitz. 241–247)

This fiery "Aithon" has turned the queen to water. And the *pathos* of Penelope's lament is heightened since the object of her lamentation sits beside her. Odysseus, meanwhile, by *dolos*, guile, (212) hides his tears.

Penelope, to confirm that this man knew her husband, asks him to describe the details of his outfit and retinue. Odysseus minutely and accurately describes these. Penelope weeps again because she has "recognized the signs" (*semat' anagnousei*, 250), the standard formulaic phrase for any scene of recognition. Here of course, the recognition is only internal or verbal: she has recognized a description. But her final object of recognition sits before her, and Homer is certainly exploiting the possibilities of *double entendres* and dramatic irony.

Odysseus then tells Penelope that he's heard Odysseus is near, and plotting revenge and destruction for the suitors. Penelope responds wishfully, though without credence: "If only this word were accomplished," she says, "then you would know love and gifts from me" (310–311). Here is another *double entendre*, as the Greek *philotes* ("love") is often a euphemism for intercourse. If the thing did occur as the beggar prophesied, there would indeed be *philotes* between her and him.

Penelope offers the beggar—whom she is ever more sympathetic toward—trundles for the night and a footbath. As Penelope asks Eurycleia to bathe the man, she comes tantalizingly close to recognition: "Bathe the man of like age to your master" (358). Eurycleia also comments on the uncanny likeness between this stranger and Odysseus (380–381). The extent of Penelope's recognition at this stage of the story has been the object of some scholarly discussion. One critic[37] has argued that Penelope in the conversation in Book XIX already recognizes her husband, and, in collusion, they are cryptically planning the death of the suitors. This has not persuaded many critics, since it would make later moments in the plot unacceptable.[38] The modern consensus sees in the colloquy of Book XIX a gradual building of "subconscious" or "intuitive" recognition between Odysseus and Penelope. Here are some instances of this critical stance:

> Penelope becomes gradually certain that the stranger is in fact her husband. But, because she has so strong a fear of making a mistake in just this situation, she cannot rationally accept her interior certainty, and her recognition therefore remains largely unconscious.[39]

...Homer, in his description of their interview in Book 19 and its aftermath in Book 20, is doing his utmost to show *both* characters in the grip of an unusually powerful unconscious tug towards the full mental union that will not be possible for several books....[40]

The goal of Book 19 is Penelope's recognition, of course, but it is a mistake to concentrate on that second when recognition is crystallized rather than on the formation of that crystal.[41]

The modern critic sees considerable psychological complexity in this scene, in which dark, half-known layers of Penelope's psyche recognize her husband, though her consciousness resists full apprehension. Meanwhile Odysseus skillfully orchestrates the re-establishment of *homophrosyne*—like-mindedness, a psychological condition—to confirm and prepare his actual self-revelation.

As Eurycleia washes the beggar's feet she glimpses the scar on his thigh. At that moment the narrative suspends and moves into a 75 line digression about the infliction of the scar. Eurycleia immediately recognizes her master: in joy she drops his foot splashing into the bucket. But before she can reveal him to all, Odysseus rather severely grabs her neck and threateningly commands her to be silent. But Penelope neither perceives nor understands (*noesai*), for Athena had turned aside her mind (*noos*).

This episode is the subject of perhaps the most well-known critical essay on the *Odyssey* in the last century, "Odysseus' Scar" by Erich Auerbach. The essay is the first chapter in a magisterial history of Western literary representation, and so is more a general reflection on Homeric narrative technique than an explication of the specific scene. All phenomena in the Homeric poems, according to Auerbach, are fully externalized "in terms perceptible to the senses" in an absolute present. The narration of this little episode is exemplary: "Clearly outlined, brightly and uniformly illuminated, men and things stand out in a realm where everything is visible."[42] When Homer digresses upon the scar, that becomes the total and fully externalized present: "What he narrates for the time being is the only present, and fills both the stage and the readers mind completely."[43]

To cite one modern critique of Auerbach, Charles Segal shows that there are elliptical and ambiguous moments even in the very episode Auerbach chooses to discuss. The "mysterious inattentiveness" of Penelope, for example, is not "a feature of self-sufficient surface lucidity." The hunting episode exhibits "mythical patterns" that are obscure and require elucidation. While Auerbach still supplies a "superb introduction" to modes of Homeric narration, even Homer's "limpidity" has "depths."

Indeed, the "foregrounded" digression has oblique moments. The story of the boar is prefaced with the story of Odysseus' naming by Autolycus, his maternal grandfather and a "swindler by Hermes' favor." Autolycus says that since he is *odyssamenos*—Fitzgerald translates, since "odium and distrust I've won"—let his name be Odysseus. The Greek word is ambiguous. Its root meaning is wrath or hatred, but it is syntactically unclear whether Autolycus and Odysseus are agents or patients of this wrath. W. B. Stanford has argued, based on "ethical" considerations, that the form is passive, and Odysseus the patient. Odysseus is famous for his ability to suppress and control emotion, so it would be unfitting to name him for a particularly strong feeling of wrath; and the whole course of the poem he is the object of Poseidon's wrath.[44]

The hunting episode in the extended digression, moreover, has a rich mythical resonance. In many cultures hunting is an initiatory motif: the successful hunt marks the passage into manhood. This gives Odysseus' boar hunt a second layer of meaning. It is both a scarring or physical impressing of identity, but also a ritualistic moment of maturation. Indeed the small parable of the boar fits nicely the structure of Campbell's heroic monomyth: separation, initiation, and reintegration. As such, it mimics the structure of the *Odyssey* as a whole, which is the story of a man's departure, his negotiating of a heroic identity, and his ultimate return.

Penelope, regaining her wits after Athena had turned them, relates to the stranger a dream she had. A gaggle of geese that had come to feed on her grain was violently killed by a mountain eagle. Odysseus, in the dream, tells her that he is the mountain eagle, come to avenge the suitors. The disguised Odysseus merely confirms the dreamed Odysseus' interpretation. Penelope, with a kind of folkloric reference to gates of horn and ivory, dismisses the dream as pure illusion.

The chief interpretive difficulty of the dream is Penelope's joy at feeding the geese, and lamentation at the slaughter. If the geese do represent the suitors, these emotions would contradict her constantly stated ones. Perhaps, as Russo has suggested, the endless flattering and blandishments of the suitors—and her own consequent *kleos*—has delighted some hidden urge. Her continued reluctance to believe the prophesies also point to a method of psychic defense: Odysseus' return would cause a major shift in identity. She has defined herself in terms of her husband's absence for so long that his sudden reappearance could constitute a significant trauma. Perhaps the cry of lamentation signifies that trauma.

As if at once to deny and admit the imminence of her husband's return, she proposes a contest: if any suitor can string Odysseus' bow and shoot an arrow through 12 aligned axeheads, she will marry him.

Book XX
In Book XX, the suitors begin their final meal. Odysseus and Penelope pass troubled nights—he on the floor, she in their bed—and when they next sleep they will be together. Books 20–23 present the coherent action of a single day; the narrative will now build toward its climax.

Odysseus lies unsleeping, "pondering" the difficulties that await him the following day. He is enraged to see a flock of serving-women shuffle out to sleep with the suitors, but battles his urge to violence. He tosses in his sheets like a *gaster*—belly, here the casing of a sausage—being turned by a cook. The *gaster*—as we have seen—emblemizes Odysseus' untypicalness as a Homeric hero. Athena comes to reassure Odysseus and pours sleep over his eyes.

As Odysseus goes under, Penelope wakes up, wailing. "It is important to note that there is a striking complementarity in the physiological and psychological rhythms."[45] She prays to Artemis to take her life, so that she might reunite with her husband in death. She has dreamt that she saw a "likeness" of her husband. She rejoiced because she thought the apparition real. Odysseus hears the queen's voice half-asleep: and "it seemed in his heart (*thumos*) that she knew him and stood near" (93–94). Poised between sleep and wakefulness, Odysseus fantasizes about the completion of his morbid task. Russo argues that though Homer's Greek lacked the precise terminology for this moment, it is a "psychopompic" (coming out of sleep) fantasy, which is a kind of precognition.[46] The psychological similarities between Odysseus and Penelope at this moment in the story are remarkable.

Odysseus slips outside in the dawn and prays to Zeus for a sign. Lightning rumbles from the clear sky, and an old women grinding flour, toiling for the suitors' bread, prays for their death. Odysseus rejoices.

As the servants busy themselves with preparing the hall for the suitors, Melanthius issues a final insult, which again Odysseus endures in silence. In marked contrast, a loyal cowherd named Philoitius introduces himself and kindly welcomes the stranger. As Eumaeus had previously, he prays for his master's return.

After the suitors enter Odysseus' hall and begin their profligate slaughtering and drinking, Telemachus commands them to stop maltreating the guest. They bite their lips at his heightened boldness.

While the suitors riot in the halls, public heralds are preparing a festival:

Now public heralds wound through Ithaca
leading a file of beasts for sacrifice, and islanders
gathered under the shade trees of Apollo,
in the precinct of the Archer ... (Fitz. 302–305)

Several ancient and modern commentators[47] have linked this festival with a celebration of the coming of spring. The word *nostos* etymologically means the return to light, and here Odysseus returns to drag Ithaca out of the darkness of its long winter. Austin writes: "The arrival of the hero, who is both beggar and itinerant "poet," signals the end of disintegration and the beginning of reconstruction."[48] Austin calls the *Odyssey* a *Chelidonismos*: a "swallow song" to commemorate the coming of spring. Northrop Frye speculated that origins of comedy lay in the victory of the new year over the old, the return of spring to thaw winter and restore life. The *Odyssey* celebrates such a victory.[49]

Athena, then, contrives a last act of insolence for the suitors: A rich and arrogant suitor, Ctesippus, casts a cow's foot at Odysseus. Having deftly ducked the blow, Odysseus smiles "sardonically"—the Greek is *sardonion* (whence the English word), which probably derives from the root *sar-*, to bear one's teeth. "The image is that of lips drawn tightly and crookedly back in a kind of suppressed snarl."[50] It is Odysseus' first smile in the *Odyssey*, and so is an important nonverbal gesture. Odysseus had smiled inwardly—"in his heart" (9.413)—when he outwitted the Cyclops, and there are obvious parallels between the two episodes.[51] Each sarcastically promised Odysseus a *xeinion*—guest-gift—which turned out to be an insult or an act of violence. Each perverts the demands of hospitality and is ultimately avenged. He signals his victory over the Cyclops, the triumph of his *metis*, with an inward smile. In the episode with Ctesippus, the smile also, if more subtly, signifies the success of his *metis*: his disguise has worked and the slaughter is near.

Telemachus finally lashes out authoritatively against the continued violence. Agalaos rejoins that the violence could end, if Penelope would but choose a husband. Telemachus says that there is no longer impediment.

Here the suitors are gripped with a foreign and unquenchable laughter, which passes into a phantasmagoric hysteria. They wheeze and weep, while their meat is defiled with blood. The image of defiled meat is familiar: when

Odysseus' crew had slaughtered the cattle of the sun, the roast meat lowed on the spits. The suitors and Odysseus' crew are linked in that their transgressions fundamentally involve food: the crew eat the sacred cattle; the suitors consume Odysseus' livestock. And Odysseus will pay them pack like the vengeful sun god. In Theoclymenus' cryptically uttered prophecy, the sun disappears: "Night shrouds you to the knees... the sun is quenched in heaven, foul mist hems us in..." (Fitz. 396–401). The darkness announces the displeasure of the cosmos.

The suitors disregard the seer, while Telemachus fixes his gaze on his father, waiting for their moment.

Book XXI
Athena "lays it upon Penelope's heart" (1) to bring the bow and the axe-heads to the suitors. As the narrative accelerates toward its end, Athena is increasingly the author of action. Many emotions, thoughts, and activities are directed by her will. This fact increases our sense of divine involvement and moral righteousness of the revenge of Odysseus, who does, after all, slaughter an entire generation of Ithacan youth.

Penelope describes her contest to the suitors, and the prize for the victor: to lead her away in marriage. She does promise a sort of fidelity to the house of Odysseus, however: she will cling to it in memory (*memnesesthai*), though only a "dream" (79). Her memory belongs to Odysseus, and so she has promised at least a fidelity that is mental, mnemic, if not physical.

Telemachus is the first to essay the bow. After three failed attempts, he bends it far enough to string, but he is checked by a silent gesture from Odysseus: "But Odysseus nodded and restrained him, though he was eager" (129). The nod (*aneneue*) is the gesture associated with Zeus' authority, and here Odysseus uses it to assert the authority of the father.

Telemachus and Odysseus have both returned to redefine their roles in the *oikos* and to reassert their male authority,[52] but this authority is, at times, in conflict. If Telemachus were to string the bow it would rob Odysseus of his patriarchal power and *kleos*. As the critic Simon Goldhill writes,

Generational continuity, however, is associated with generational conflict; the authority of the father opposing the growing awareness of the son of his own potency which is not commensurate with his position of inferior standing in the hierarchy of the *oikos*....[53]

Odysseus prevents Telemachus from undermining him as father. From Penelope, the specific threat of female infidelity would also undermine his authority: female sexual license threatens the patrilineal continuity of the *oikos*.[54]

A suitor feebly tries to string the great bow, but lacks the vigor to bend it. Meanwhile, Eumaeus and Philoitius—two faithful servants—wander discouraged outside. Odysseus slyly follows them out and reveals himself, enlisting their help in the impending fight. The scene shares some of the formulaic aspects and phrases of recognition scenes, but, as we have already seen, the means of revelation and recognition vary significantly with the type of relationship being reconstructed: Telemachus must accept the authority of the father; subordinate servants are persuaded by the revelation of the *sema* of the scar; Argos, the dog, is granted a totally non-semiotic recognition. Penelope and Laertes, we will see, require more complex, personal, and unseen *semata* (signs) to verify the identity of Odysseus.

Eurymachus is the next suitor to try to string the bow, but he too lacks the strength. Antinous then proposes they postpone the contest until after the holiday. All the suitors readily consent.

Odysseus then rises and requests a try. Antinous rudely refuses him, but Penelope interposes: she insists that the stranger—a *xenos* of Telemachus—get his wish. Telemachus then sends her back to her room and her loom, insisting that the *kratos* (power) of the household belongs to him. She complies.

Eumaeus, over the sneers of the suitors, delivers the bow to Odysseus. Telemachus threatens them for their misbehavior, but they break into another frenzied, demonic laughter.

Odysseus takes up the bow, slowly studying it, looking for damage. Homer offers one of his most memorable similes to ennoble this climax:

> But the man skilled in all ways of contending,[55]
> satisfied by the bow's look and heft,
> like a musician, like a harper, when
> with a quiet hand upon his instrument
> he draws between his thumb and forefinger
> a sweet new string upon a peg: so effortlessly
> Odysseus in one motion strung the bow.
> Then slid his right hand down the cord and plucked it,
> so the taut gut vibrating hummed and sang
> a swallow's note. (Fitz. 460–469)

Odysseus himself composes the four central books of the *Odyssey*, and, uniquely in Homer, is the poet of his own *kleos*. He is displaced from his achievement in Troy, a world which has already become fixed and immutable, the object of epic song. Here on the very cusp of his second great moment of achievement, he once again becomes a musician as he enters heroic action. This miraculous alchemy is at the root of all heroic poetry: to change a human into a song.

Homer is specific about the type of note Odysseus' bow produces: "like the voice of a swallow" (411). The song of the swallow—the *Chelidonismos*—is associated with the return of spring, and the bird-like note that emanates from Odysseus' instrument celebrates such a restoration of life and order.

The suitors stare dumbly in the hall, as portentous thunder claps above. Odysseus nocks an arrow and shoots it cleanly through the 12 iron axe-heads. Odysseus tells Telemachus: "The hour has come to cook their lordships' mutton—| supper by daylight. Other amusements later, | with song and harping that adorn a feast" (Fitz. 492–495). The feast to which Odysseus refers, of course, is the slaughter of the suitors. Before the first shot is launched is the darkly ironic suggestion of anthropophagy. The suitors, who slaughtered so many of

Odysseus' animals for their meals, are about to be slaughtered themselves.

Book XXII

Odysseus pours the arrows out of his quiver at his feet, and nocks one for Antinous. Antinous obliviously sips a festal cup of wine as an arrow punctures his throat up to the feathers. "The rhetorical question... and the reference to Antinous' 'tender throat'... are doubtless intended by the poet to suggest that death when it comes to prince at the acme of his golden youth is sad and pitiful no matter how villainous the dying man may be. The poet retains an equanimity and humaneness above the passions of his characters.... It is in such techniques that Homer's greatness of spirit and technique is revealed."[56]

The suitors imagine that this was some errant arrow, and not purposeful vengeance. Homer calls the "fools" for this miscalculation: *nepioi*. The same word is applied to the reckless companions in the first lines of the poem. They are *nepioi* for eating the cattle of the sun. The suitors and companions are linked textually and thematically. Both groups of fools transgress in culinary ways, and both incur deadly divine visitations for it.

Odysseus reveals himself, though never mentions his name: "You never thought I'd come home from the land of Troy" (35). There is no emphatic pronouncement of his name, as he had done for the Phaeacians, nor does Eurymachus admit decisively that he is indeed Odysseus: "If you are Odysseus of Ithaca come back..." (45). The classicist Sheila Murnaghan writes of this moment: "While its central action is the removal of disguise, it is devoid of recognition."[57] It is the suitors' central and deadly failure that they never recognize Odysseus through his disguise. The full process of recognition involves a readoption by Odysseus of his socially determined role. The suitors are incapable of this, and so incapable of a full recognition. They only recognize Odysseus when they are dead in Hades, in Book XXIV.

Eurymachus offers Odysseus reparations for lost property to try to quench his wrath, but the king darkly refuses: "Not for all the treasure of your fathers, | all you enjoy, lands, flocks, or any gold | put up by others, would I hold my hand" (Fitz. 64–66). Readers familiar with the *Iliad* will recall Achilles' response to Agamemnon's similar attempt at redress: "Not even if he should give to me as many gifts as there are grains of sand and dust would Agamemnon persuade my fighting spirit" (Il. 9.385–386). Odysseus' attitude clearly echoes Achilles': no material wealth could repay the dishonor. It heightens the irony of this textual connection that Achilles' words in the *Iliad* are spoken to Odysseus as Agamemnon's emissary. The response feels inconsonant with some of Odysseus' core *ethos*: he stands for pragmatism and equanimity, while his crafty intelligence is often applied to some gain (*kerdos*). Odysseus here, in his battle-lust, adopts certain types of behavior that properly belong to Achilles.

Book XXII is the most Iliadic book of the *Odyssey*: an intransigent hero displays his martial valor, and Homer renders his *aristeia*—day of greatness—in violent detail. There are some crucial differences from Iliadic modes of fighting: Odysseus is hugely outnumbered by his foes, who have been deprived of arms, and he begins the struggle with a bow, a less heroic weapon than the spear or sword. Despite these differences, the linguistic and narrative atmosphere is overwhelmingly reminiscent of the *Iliad*. Textual echoes abound. For instance, after Odysseus refuses his entreaties, Eurymachus implores the suitors to oppose him: "Fight, I say, | let's remember the joy of it (*charme*)" (Fitz. 78–79). The word *charme*—usually translated "joy of battle"—occurs 22 times in the *Iliad*, but occurs only here in the entire *Odyssey*. Book XXII, in its very language, evokes and invokes the tradition of the *Iliad*.

Eurymachus lunges at Odysseus, who sends an arrow through his chest. Bread, wine, and gore mingle on the floor. Amphinomus charges next, but he is lanced from behind by a spear from Telemachus. The order that the suitors and other retainers are killed is deliberate and meaningful. "The punishments meted out to the various groups who have exploited the hero's long absence seem very precisely and appropriately graded."[58] The strongest but also most culpable of the suitors is killed first (Antinous), and each thereafter is killed according to a hierarchical rank. As Jenny Clay has noted, this hierarchy corresponds to their position at the feast (*dais*) around the table: "The massacre of the suitors progresses... from the highest, Antinous and Eurymachus, on down to Leodes, and reproduces with grisly humor the order of the *dais*.... In the *dais* of death, they all receive their just desserts."[59]

Telemachus retrieves the arms they had hidden in the storeroom, but unwittingly leaves the door open. Melanthius is able to climb in through the open door and provide arms to the suitors. Going back a second time, Melanthius is apprehended by Eumaeus and Philoitius, who suspend his contorted body from the ceiling.

Athena appears in the guise of Mentor to assist the effort. She turns herself into a swallow and flutters up to the rafters. Here is another reference to a swallow: the cosmic force of spring aligns itself with Odysseus.

The suitors try to coordinate their spear throws, but the shafts are all diverted by Athena. After a flurry of kills by Odysseus and his allies, a hovering image of Athena's great aegis takes shape in the hall. The suitors madly cower and scamper, like "cows stung by gadflies." Some modern readers are bothered by the abundance of help that Odysseus receives from the gods, and Athena in particular, as if divine aid detracted from the greatness or achievement of Odysseus. "An Odysseus who should conquer without divine aid would be nearly meaningless. What is at stake for Homer is rather more than the heroic triumph of his Odysseus; behind this, or rather *in* this, there is the triumph of Order over Disorder."[60] The divine presence universalizes and validates Odysseus' action.

When the suitors are slain, and "torn men moan at death, and blood runs smoking over the whole floor" (Fitz. 348), the seer Leodes supplicates himself before Odysseus: "I clasp your knees, Odysseus," he says. "Respect me and have pity on me" (312). This is an exact quotation, with the name changed, of a scene at the end of the *Iliad* in which Lycaon supplicates himself to Achilles (*Il.* 21.73–74). Both heroes mercilessly kill the suppliants. The allusion—as the other Iliadic references that multiply in this book—places Odysseus in comparison with his epic precursor, and emphasizes his heroic valor in the mode of Achilles. The heroes' responses to the suppliants, moreover, illustrate important differences between them.[61] Achilles says that he will no longer spare life since his companion, Patroclus, is dead:

> So, friend, you die also. Why all this clamor about it?
> Patroklos is also dead, who was better by far than you are.
> Do you not see what a man I am...?
> Yet even I have also my death...
> (Lattimore *Il.* 21.106–110)

Of this response the German critic Walter Burkert writes: "There is no irony in this word ["friend"], but only an uncanny [*unheimlich*] amphiboly: the connection linking Achilles with Lycaon is a solidarity in death for death."[62] Lycaon appealed to Achilles' sense of pity for their common fate as humans; for Achilles the community of death does not inspire restraint, but rather maddens him for ever more ferocious killing. Odysseus' response to Leodes, by contrast, addresses his *nostos*:

> You were a diviner in this crowd? How often
> you must have prayed my sweet day of return
> would never come ... (Fitz. 361–363)

The community of death impels Achilles to murder, but Odysseus is maddened by any interference with his "sweet return" (*glukus nostos*). This is a fundamental difference between them.

After Odysseus beheads Leodes, the bard Phemios supplicates himself. Were Odysseus to kill him, he explains, it would be a grief (*akhos*) later. Odysseus decides mercifully to preserve the poet, the gesture which guarantees that his *kleos* will resonate in the future. He can only achieve his full heroic apotheosis in a future song, and so the bard is vital to his success.

When death has been distributed to the feasters, Odysseus calls out Eurycleia, who cries out in triumph. Odysseus commands that she not exult over the slain: death is never cause for celebration; he was an instrument of heaven, not a vigilante avenger. Odysseus asks her to lead the "harlots" out: those of his serving-women who had lain with the suitors. He forces these to wash the gore and carry out the corpses. Then Telemachus hangs them all—a particularly ignominious and humiliating death. Finally, the perfidious goatherd Melanthius receives the most grisly treatment of all.

Odysseus instructs his servants to purify the hall with sulfur and fire. The servants then gather round Odysseus, kissing and embracing him. The hero of *metis* has finally unmasked himself; he is overcome by "sweet longing" and by crying.

Book XXIII
Eurycleia eagerly wakes Penelope to tell her the happy news, but Penelope, hard and incredulous as ever, dismisses her as mad. She is upset to be torn from sleep: she had not slept so soundly, she explains, since her Odysseus sailed off 20 years prior. Sleep is an ambivalent boon in the *Odyssey*: on the one hand, it is a lapse of mind and heroic failure that permits Odysseus' mutinous crew to loose the winds of Aeolus and slaughter the cattle of the sun. On the other hand, it has the strong suggestion of awakening into new life: Odysseus was asleep when the Phaeacians conveyed him home to his Ithaca at last, and Penelope has just slumbered through the climax of the epic, the restoration of her husband as king. Sleep is the primal and death-like "whence" of the heroic journey. Douglas Frame has suggested that *nostos* (homecoming) is linked etymologically to *noos* (mind),[63] postulating that both derive from an ancient root *nes-* meaning "return to light and life." In this etymological light, one could define *nostos* as waking into mindfulness, which explains the thematic import of sleep.

As Eurycleia persists, Penelope staunchly refuses to believe. It must be a god, she says, who has come down to repay the suitors' outrages. Odysseus has the aura of divinity—or at least divine sanction—elsewhere in the *Odyssey*. Telemachus, for example, had also compared his father to a god in Book XVI. An anonymous suitor in Book XVII, after Odysseus was struck by a stool, speculated that he might be a disguised god:

> A poor show, that—hitting this famished tramp—
> bad business, if he happened to be a god.
> You know they go in foreign guise, the gods do,
> looking like strangers, turning up
> in towns and settlements to keep an eye
> on manners, good or bad. (Fitz. 633–637)

Emily Kearns has argued that the "the moral climate of the poem is precisely that of a theoxeny"[64]—that is, a disguised god who has come to test and punish human hubris. Penelope's response to Eurycleia heightens our sense of this "moral climate."

When Eurycleia ushers her out into the *megaron*, Penelope stands in frozen awe gazing at Odysseus. At one moment she can recognize her husband; and then she sees only a stranger befouled by blood. As she stands dumbly, Telemachus asks her how she could be so hard not to embrace her husband after twenty years of separation.

If this really is Odysseus, she responds, she will know him better than anyone else: there are "secret signs" (*semata kekrummena*, 110) known to them alone. Their encrypted knowledge reaffirms and defines them as lovers—they know what is hidden from others, what's on the inside. The *sema* that effects their final recognition is the configuration of the bed in the hidden, innermost chamber of the house, known only to them and one loyal maid. Odysseus feels the sting of infidelity when he fears someone else has shared that secret knowledge of the bedroom.

Odysseus smiles at Penelope's response. Odysseus then devises a stratagem to avoid the detection of the mass slaughter by angry families who might seek requital. He commands the harper to strum a festive tune, so that any passers by will think there is a wedding ceremony occurring. That way, he says, "the report (*kleos*) of the slaughter of the suitors won't spread widely through the town." The complex entanglement of meanings signified by the word *kleos* is evident here: at once the fame or glory of the warrior, the report or rumor of human action, and the medium of song through which that fame is preserved. Furthermore, Odysseus' ironic involvement with *kleos* is evident here: he uses a bard not to preserve but to disguise the report of his valor. "Yet even this concealment adds to the *Odyssey*'s praise of Odysseus as *polumetis*, as the man canny enough to achieve this particular, remarkable victory."[65] On display here, then, is Odysseus' ability to manipulate his own *kleos* in order to augment it in the future.

Penelope leads Odysseus toward the inner bedroom, and he is outwitted by Penelope's ruse to test him: Seeing his old bedroom he erupts in anger: "Who dared to move my bed?" (Fitz. 209). He then describes how he made it: cutting away the branches of the olive tree, smoothing the timber, stretching the ox-hide. Hearing this, Penelope's heart "dissolves" as she recognizes the sure signs (*semata empeda*, 205–206).

What exactly is the *sema*? What does Penelope recognize? It is not anything so external as a scar or a face. It is, rather, an emotional outburst and a memory narrated. He is outraged at the hint of betrayal and remembers in full detail the construction of the bed.

If for Eurycleia and the two loyal herdsman the scar was enough to confirm Odysseus' identity, with Penelope the *semata* are inscribed much deeper. Odysseus had wished *homophrosyne*—like-mindedness—for Nausikaa in her future relationships, and here Homer enacts this prayer for us. Recognition occurs in and by the mind. For Odysseus and Penelope, it is a question of the interior, the hidden (*kekrummena*). Because without a shared memory, every *sema* is polysemous.

Penelope tells him she was only testing him; no one else has seen the bed; she is faithful still. Odysseus, weeping, clasps his "darling wife" in his arms—his *alokhon thumarea* (232). Etymologically, an *alokhon* is "one who shares the same bed" and *thumarea* means "befitting one's *thumos*." The phrase occurs one other time in Homer: Achilles uses it to describe

Briseis, the slave girl whom Agamemnon bereaved him of at the beginning of the *Iliad*. Penelope, too, grasps Odysseus:

> As welcome as when land appears to men swimming,
> whose ship Poseidon smashes in the sea, as it is driven
> by wind and wave, and few have fled from the hoary
> water to land by swimming, and much brine is
> congealed on their body; joyfully they have set foot on
> land, fleeing evil—so most welcome to her was her
> husband as she gazed at him, and she would not release
> his neck from her white arms. (233–240)

Here is the final of the *Odyssey*'s "reverse similes," and here, I believe, its purpose is not to indicate the social order is somehow disturbed and upset, as in Helene Foley's argument, but rather the restoration of husband and wife to mental oneness. It is as if their emotional lives have become interchangeable—she warding off the lupine and rapacious suitors, he wracked in the ocean and sojourning among temptresses, demons, and giants. Their emotions are described *in terms of* the other; they are transposed into each other's similes.

Athena stays the sun below the ocean to extend the night for love and storytelling. But Odysseus has a sad duty unfulfilled: he must leave again, he tells his wife, and plant an oar in a foreign place where they know neither salt not navigation, in order to propitiate Poseidon. "One perilous voyage ended only begins another," wrote Herman Melville, and now that Odysseus has achieved his heart's desire, returned to the small room at the center of his home, he is forced again to be a centrifugal hero.

After he confides in her, they come together in their old bed. Two great ancient Alexandrian critics of Homer, Aristarchus and Aristophanes, called line 256 (Fitz. 332) the *telos* or *peras*—end or limit—of the *Odyssey*. Many critics of the Analyst school—who believe many passages of our Homer texts to be interpolations of later editors and compilers—have taken this as an invitation to obelize the rest of the *Odyssey*. Several have analyzed the morphology and vocabulary of the last 600 lines to show that it could not be the same as Homer, but such linguistic studies are indecisive.[66] Other critics have suggested that the Greek *telos* need not necessarily mean "end," but can also mean "consummation" or "fulfillment," and so we are not obliged to interpret the ancient critics too rigidly. Odysseus and Penelope reunited in bed could certainly be the "end" in this more figurative sense. Other critics have justly pointed out that there are too many elements of the story still unresolved for the epic to end here: Odysseus must reunite with his father, and either destroy or appease the suitors' families who will be eager to avenge their sons and brothers. There may be something dissatisfying about the *Odyssey*'s denouement after the emotional intensity of the scenes between Odysseus and Penelope, and an *Odyssey* that ended at line 296 might fit our preconception of the proper shape of a love story. But one should be careful not to confuse the teleology of the modern love story with ancient epic.

Penelope and Odysseus delight in love and storytelling, "speaking to each other" (301). The verb of discourse, here, is *enepein*. The first words of the *Odyssey* itself are *andra moi ennepe mousa*: the verb of speech used in the invocation of the Muse is the same used here, making this connubial storytelling curiously parallel to the epic as a whole. Penelope's story is told first, how she had warded off the arrogant suitors. Her adventures, like Odysseus', are introduced by the epic verb *enepein* (the word "epic" derives from the same *ep-* root present in the verb), indicating that she too has accomplished heroic feats, worthy of *kleos*. Furthermore, the repetition of *enepein* suggests a *mise-en-abyme*, a term from literary theory denoting a work that somehow depicts its own creation. Could Odysseus be narrating the *Odyssey* in bed?

Odysseus tells Penelope he must find his father, warning her to stay quietly in her inner chambers since the angry kin of the suitors will be vengeful. He wakes Telemachus and tells him to arm. Athena leads them out of town, covering them in night. (372).

Book XXIV

Hermes conducts the souls of the suitors into the underworld, who "squeak like bats falling in the depths of a cavernous cave" (5–7). There, they meet Agamemnon and Achilles—the two other paradigms of male achievement and *kleos* in Homer. Achilles reflects that Agamemnon, though he marshaled so great an army, was robbed of his rightful *kleos* by his most pitiful death. The craven ambush of Aegisthus and Clytemnestra effaced years of martial glory. The stated goal of a Homeric hero is to be a song to future generations (see, for example, *Od.* 3.203–204, 24.296–298). Accordingly, a life ought to have the same pleasing shape (*morphe*) as song. The various forms of death confirm or prevent this.

Agamemnon, then, contrasts his death to Achilles'. He calls Achilles "blessed," because he died in Troy. The armies warred around his body for a full day, while a dust-cloud obscured his corpse. Agamemnon describes the various splendors of Achilles' funeral, including a threnody from the nine Muses themselves. For Achilles, then, and the mode of greatness he represents, the Muses are *eulogists*: they can only sing, and his *kleos* can only materialize, after death. Similarly, Agamemnon tells Achilles: "Though you perished your name did not: your *kleos* will be among all men forever" (93–94). Achilles' *kleos*, in both the *Iliad* and the *Odyssey*, is only referred to in the future tense. Odysseus, however, can refer to his own *kleos* in the present tense: "My *kleos* reaches the heavens" (9.20). As a hero who is *polumetis*, "of many wiles," one of Odysseus' primary strategies is to obscure, manipulate, or marshal this *kleos* to his own ends.

Book XXIV, then, is another locus of contrast between Odysseus and Achilles, and the competing visions of *kleos* they embody. This contrast is drawn admirably by Anthony Edwards:

> In setting Achilles up as an emblem of the heroic, the *Iliad* ennobles and mythicizes the hero's death, and sees in the premature destruction of strength and youth their moment of greatest beauty.... The *Odyssey*, by

contrast, both narrates and embodies a *kleos* that rather is lost through death. It is a *kleos* for survival, and the *kleos* and *nostos* this survival entails. It is a *kleos* which can be won through *xenia* and revenge. It is a *kleos* which cannot be claimed by a single individual on the margins of society, but must be shared by husband and wife as a sign of mutual commitment and the integrity of the social world.[67]

Achilles' heroism is powerfully agonistic, and *agon* in the *Iliad* is a destructive and alienating force. Odysseus, by contrast, must sublimate his *agon*, because his *kleos* demands cooperation, integration, and interdependence.

As Hermes leads in the souls of the suitors, Agamemnon recognizes and questions Amphinomus.[68] Amphinomus narrates the story of return and revenge, with a few mistakes and misperceptions that expose the continuing ignorance and mis-recognition of the suitors.[69] When Agamemnon hears of Odysseus' happy *nostos*, he launches into an encomium to Penelope. "How well she remembered Odysseus," he claims, while his wife is a symbol of female treachery and faithlessness everywhere. Faithfulness and good memory are closely allied. "The *kleos* of her *arête* will never perish," he continues (196–197).[70] This is a highly heroic (and male) figuration, here applied to Penelope: the "fame of one's excellence" would usually refer to violent exploits. The praise of Penelope, situated here, calls attention to the mutual interdependence of husband and wife in attaining *kleos*.

The story returns to Odysseus, who has wandered off to the orchard in search of his father. Characteristically, he decides to dissimulate and not to reveal himself fully right away. He fabricates another false history in which he entertained Odysseus as a guest-friend. Laertes wails in lamentation; the stranger has reopened a sore wound. Then Odysseus relents: "I myself right here am that man," Odysseus says. That is a (somewhat cumbersome) English translation of what is a simple Greek sentence: "*keinos hod' ego*" (321). *Keinos* is the most distant deictic pronoun in Greek, referring to an antecedent that is usually absent (a more emphatic form of English "that"). *Hod'* is the deictic pronoun of presence, like English "this here." And *ego* means "I." So a longer rendering of this sentence might read: I, standing right before you, am that man just evoked in language. This strategy of mixed deixis—a "that" becoming a "this"—is common to Odysseus.

He evokes a heroic persona that is thought to be absent in language or song, and then makes a startling epiphany. Among the Phaeacians, for example, he asked Demodocus to sing the sack of Troy and his brilliant ruse of the horse, just before telling his name. The uncanny effect of Odysseus' revelations is the sudden appearance of a figure just conjured in language. The strange sequence of pronouns, conflating absence and presence, renders this sense.

Laertes is incredulous, and demands some *sema* to confirm his identity. First Odysseus shows the scar, and remembers the occasion of its infliction. Then he shares his simple memory of walking the orchard with Laertes, only a small boy, as his father named the trees and handed down a number of trees. Laertes—just as Penelope had—feints in his joy, "recognizing the secure signs" (346). The same metaphoric complexity of the word *empeda* (secure) that Froma Zeitlin showed in the recognition scene with Penelope obtains here: the sign is *empeda*—secure, trustworthy—but also *empeda* in the literal, etymological sense: "rooted firmly in the ground." The security or "rootedness" of this orchard, furthermore, is precisely what is challenged by the suitors and Odysseus' absence: the pattern of patrilineal inheritance. The boyhood memory of Odysseus is a moment of enculturation and succession, regained by his sudden appearance at home and authorized by his father's recognition. Giving a "secure sign," he has won back his "firmly rooted" land.

Laertes and Odysseus, after a teary embrace, rejoin the others to share a meal. Meanwhile, the news (the *kleos*) of the killings has spread through the town. Eupeithes, father of Antinous, justly points out that Odysseus is responsible for exterminating two generations of Ithacan youth, and rallies an angry throng to arms. Medon and an old seer try to dissuade the crowd, arguing that the hand of god was in Odysseus' success. But an intransigent sect follows Eupeithes.

Just as in the very beginning of the epic, Athena asks Zeus his will. He authorizes her to intervene in the coming skirmish. Zeus says he will make the townsmen oblivious of their slain sons and brothers: Zeus must engineer this forced forgetting (*eklesis*, 485) to reinstall Odysseus in power. That way, he says, there will be friendship (*philia*), prosperity (*ploutos*), and peace (*eirene*) (486–487).

When they see the angry townsmen approaching, Laertes, Odysseus, Telemachus, and some retainers arm themselves. You are going into battle, Odysseus tells his son, "where the best (*aristoi*) are distinguished. Do not bring shame on the race of your fathers" (507-8). The emphasis is on generational succession. Old Laertes cries out: "Ah, what a day for me dear gods! | to see my son and grandson vie in courage" (Fitz. 571–572). This is the perfect image of patrilineal continuity restored: three generations of men on the battle field. Laertes kills Eupeithes with the hurl of a spear before Athena appears—in the guise of Mentor—to stop the fighting. Both parties swear an eternal pact of peace.

An epic that ended in Book XXIII would lack this final image of the continuity of family and heirs. Odysseus' *nostos* is a "return to humanity in the broadest sense," as Charles Segal wrote, from the fabulous monsters and divinities of the wanderings to wife, family, and orchard; from the offer of immortality to the reality of death but the solace of a son. The return does not end in bed with Penelope—love is not foremost in the hierarchy of emotions, as it is for us. It is rather a craving for order, for stability, that drives Odysseus, which can only exist within the *oikos*: once you venture too far outside, you are in the world of guile, of war, of lies, dissimulation, giants, whirlpools, pirates, shifting identities and the pitiless sea. It is only in his return, his reintegration into human relations, into family, into political life, in short, into the *oikos*, that Odysseus can finally become the *Odyssey*'s riddling theme: *andra*.

—Thomas Schmidt

Notes

1. Quotations from the *Odyssey* come from Fitzgerald's translation or W.B. Stanford's two-volume Greek edition. All quotations from Fitzgerald are attributed, with line numbers that refer to his translation; all other quotations are my translations.

2. H. D. F. Kitto, "The *Odyssey*: The Exclusion of Surprise," in *The Odyssey: Modern Critical Interpretations*, ed. Harold Bloom (Chelsea House, 1988), 17

3. For more on Penelope's *kleos*, see Book XXIV.

4. Gilbert Rose, "The Quest of Telemachus," *TAPA* 98 (1967) 391–398

5. William S. Anderson, "Calypso and Elysium," *CJ* 54 (1958) 4

6. *Ibid.* 5

7. Jean-Pierre Vernant, "The Refusal of Odysseus," in Schein (1996) 189

8. George Dimock, "The Name of Odysseus," *Hudson Review* 9.1 (1956), 52–70 [reprinted in *Essays on the* Odyssey: *Selected Modern Criticism*, ed. Charles H. Taylor (Bloomington: Indiana University Press, 1963)]

9. Thomas van Nortwick, "Penelope and Nausicaa," *TAPA* 109 (1979) 269–276

10. *Ibid.* 271

11. Detienne and Vernant, *Cunning Intelligence in Greek Society and Culture*, 5

12. The etymology and this quote come from George E. Dimock, Jr., "The Epic of Suffering and Fulfillment," in *Homer's Odyssey: A Critical Handbook*, ed. Conny Nelson, 165

13. Goldhill, *The Poet's Voice*, 47

14. Robert Schmiel, "Achilles in Hades," *CP* 82.1 (1987), 37

15. Pietro Pucci, "The Song of the Sirens," in *The Song of the Sirens: Essays on Homer*, 1–9.

16. Charles Segal, *Singers, Heroes, and Gods in the* Odyssey (Ithaca, NY: Cornell University Press, 1994) 100

17. *Ibid.* 105

18. *Ibid.*

19. This whole analysis of the episode of the cattle borrows heavily from Norman Austin, *Archery at the Dark of the Moon*.

20. See Norman Austin, *Archery at the Dark of the Moon*, Chapter 3.

21. *Poetics* 1459B

22. Food as an area of transgression, and the perverted *dais*, were important subjects of discussion in Prof. Egbert Bakker's graduate seminar on the *Odyssey* at Yale University, Fall, 2005. It would be impossible to trace my indebtedness here, but let it suffice to say that my thoughts on this subject are in large part derived from him and my peers.

23. Segal, 183

24. Jean Starobinski, "The Inside and the Outside," *The Hudson Review* 17 (1975) 347

25. Segal, 181–182
26. Charles Segal, *Singers, Heroes, and Gods in the* Odyssey, 172–3
27. Goldhill (1991) 9
28. Goldhill (1991) 11
29. Pietro Pucci, *Odysseus Polutropos*
30. Goldhill (1991) 43
31. Pucci (1987) 162
32. Kitto, "The *Odyssey*: The Exclusion of Surprise," in Bloom (1988) 29. Gregory Nagy discusses how the Irus episode parodies features of "blame poetry" (as opposed to praise or *kleos* poetry). See Nagy (1979) 222ff.
33. For a discussion of the significance of this laugh, see Daniel B. Levine, "Penelope's Laugh: *Odyssey* 18.163." *AJP* 104 (1983): 172–178
34. Quoted in Uvo Hölscher, "Penelope and the Suitors," in Schein (1996) 135
35. *Ibid.* 136
36. Helene P. Foley, "'Reverse Similes' and Sex Roles in the *Odyssey*," reprinted in Bloom (1988) 87–101
37. Philip Whaley Harsh, "Penelope and Odysseus in Odyssey XIX," *AJP* 71 (1950) 1–21.
38. See Russo (1983) 7n.
39. A. Amory, "The Reunion of Odysseus and Penelope," in *Essays on the Odyssey: Selected Modern Criticism*, ed. C. H. Taylor, 105
40. Joseph Russo, "Interview and Aftermath: Dream, Fantasy, and Intuition in *Odyssey* 19 and 20," *AJP* 103 (1982) 6
41. Norman Austin, *Archery at the Dark of the Moon: Poetic Problems in Homer's* Odyssey (University of California Press, 1975), 224
42. Erich Auerbach, *Mimesis: The Representation of Reality in Western Literature* (Princeton, 1953 reprinted 2003) 3
43. *Ibid.* 3–4. Auerbach discusses Homeric representation in contradistinction to representation in the Old Testament, where narrative is "elliptical" and "vertical."
44. W. B. Stanford, "The Homeric Etymology of the Name Odysseus," *CP* 47 (1952) 209–13
45. Russo (1982) 12
46. *Ibid.* 16
47. See Austin (1975) 246
48. Austin (1975) 250
49. *Ibid.*
50. See W.B. Stanford's commentary on the *Odyssey* (1996) 352.
51. Daniel B. Levine, "Odysseus' Smiles" *TAPA* 114, 4
52. See Simon Goldhill, *Language, Sexuality, Narrative: The* Oresteia (Cambridge 1984) 191
53. *Ibid*
54. This is a familiar concept in evolutionary psychology. A male's sexual jealousy is to ensure he raise a genetically related (i.e. patrilineal) child.

55. In the Greek, there is no echo of the opening line of the poem. This is Fitzgerald's invention.

56. Stanford (1958) 372. Oral-formulaic theory makes problematic some of the language of this commentary, but the core sentiment stands unscathed.

57. Sheila Murnaghan, *Disguise and Recognition in the* Odyssey, 56

58. Malcom Davies, "Odyssey 22.474-7: Murder or Mutilation?" *CQ* 44 (1994) 535

59. Jenny Strauss Clay, "The Dais of Death" *TAPA* 124 (1994) 39

60. Kitto in Bloom p. 17

61. The fullest discussion of this scene is in Pucci (1987) 127–138.

62. Quoted in Pucci (1987) 137.

63. Frame (1978) chapter 3.

64. Emily Kearns, "The Return of Odysseus: A Homeric Theoxeny," *CQ* 32 (1982) 8.

65. Goldhill (1991) 95

66. See Stanford (1962) 405 for a good (if a bit outdated) overview.

67. Anthony T. Edwards, *Achilles in the Odyssey* (Königsten, 1985) 92 [I have transliterated the Greek words]

68. This speech is the focus of many of the debates about the spuriousness of this second *nekyia*. For more on strategies of interpreting this speech, see Simon Goldhill, "Reading Differences: Juxtaposition in the *Odyssey*." *Ramus* 19 (1989).

69. Goldhill (1989)

70. The phrase is syntactically ambiguous: it could alternately be the *kleos* of her *arête* or his *arête*. This very fact of this ambiguity, I think, emphasizes their total interdependence in winning renown. Their *kleos* is one.

List of Important Greek Words

agon—contest, competition

anagnorisis—recognition

andra—man (acc., nom. *aner*)

arête—excellence, virtue

aristos—best

bie—strength, force, violence

dolos—guile

empeda—secure, grounded

gaster—belly

homophrosyne—like-mindedness

hubris—arrogance

kleos—fame, glory, renown; report, hearsay

megaron—great hall, the main room for eating or storytelling in the various households visited in the *Odyssey*, and the theater of most of its action.

metis—cunning intelligence, craftiness. And so: *polumetis*—of many wiles.

nostos—return, homecoming

oikos—home, household

polutropos—from the root *polu-*, "many," and *tropos*, "turn, way." So: of many turns, of many ways, versatile.

sema—sign

thumos—heart, spirit

xenos—stranger, guest-friend. So: *xenia*—guest-friendship

CRITICAL VIEWS

Longinus on Homer's Sublimity

Perhaps you will not think me boring, my friend, if I insert here another passage from the poet, one that treats of human affairs, to show you his habit of entering into the sublimity of his heroic theme. Darkness and helpless night suddenly descend upon his Greek army. At his wits end Ajax cries:

> Zeus Father, rescue from out of the mist the sons of
>   Achaia,
> Brighten the heaven with sunshine, grant us the
>   sight of our eyes.
> Just so it be in daylight, destroy us.[1]

These are the true feelings of an Ajax. He does not plead for his life: such a prayer would demean the hero: but since the disabling darkness robbed his courage of all noble use, therefore, distressed to be idle in battle, he prays for light on the instant, hoping thus at the worst to find a burial worthy of his courage, even though Zeus be ranged against him. Here indeed the battle is blown along by the force of Homer's writing, and he himself

> Stormily raves, as the spear-wielding War-god, or
>   Fire, the destroyer,
> Stormily raves on the hills in the deep-lying thickets of
> woodland;
> Fringed are his lips with the foam-froth[2]

Yet throughout the *Odyssey*, which for many reasons we must not exclude from our consideration, Homer shows that, as genius ebbs, it is the love of storytelling that characterizes old age. There are indeed many indications that he composed this tale after the *Iliad*; for example, through the *Odyssey* he introduces as episodes remnants of the adventures at Ilium; yes, and does he not in this poem render to his heroes their meed of lamentation as if it were something long known? In fact the Odyssey is simply an epilogue to the *Iliad*:

> There then Ajax lies, great warrior; there lies
> Achilles;
> There, too, Patroclus lies, the peer of the gods in
> counsel;
> There, too my own dear son.[3]

It was, I imagine, for the same reason that, writing the *Iliad* in the heyday of his genius he made the whole piece lively with dramatic action, whereas in the *Odyssey* narrative predominates, the characteristic of old age. So in the *Odyssey* one may liken Homer to the setting sun; the grandeur remains without the intensity. For no longer does he preserve the sustained energy of the great *Iliad* lays, the consistent sublimity which never sinks into flatness, the flood of moving incidents in quick succession, the versatile rapidity and actuality, dense with images drawn from real life. It is rather as though the Ocean had retreated into itself and lay quiet within its own confines. Henceforth we see the ebbing tide of Homer's greatness, as he wanders in the realm of the fabulous and incredible. In saying this I have not forgotten the storms in the *Odyssey* and such incidents as that of the Cyclops—I am describing old age, but the old age of a Homer—yet the fact is that in every one of these passages the mythical element predominates over the real.

I have been led into this digression to show you, as I said, that great genius with the decline of vigour often lapses very easily into nonsense—there is the story of the wineskin[4] and the men whom Circe turned into swine[5]—Zoilus called them "porkers in tears"—there is the nurturing of Zeus like a nestling by the doves,[6] Odysseus' ten days without food on the wrecked ship,[7] and the incredible story of the suitors slaying[8] Can one call these things anything but veritable dreams of Zeus?[9]

There is another justification for our considering the *Odyssey* as well as the *Iliad*. I wanted you to realize how, in great writers and poets, declining emotional power passes into character portrayals. For instance, his character sketches of the daily life in Odysseus' household constitute a sort of comedy of character.

Notes

1. *Iliad* 17.645–7.
2. *Iliad* 15.605.
3. *Odyssey* 3.109–11. Both opinions about the order of *Iliad* and *Odyssey* were held in antiquity: Seneca (*De brevitate vitae* 13) regards it as a typical example of the useless questions raised by literary scholars.
4. Aeolus imprisoned the winds in a wineskin: *Odyssey* 10.19–22.
5. *Odyssey* 10.237. Zoilus of Amphipolis—nicknamed *Homeromastix*, Scourge of Homer—was a fourth-century sophist and moralist who criticized improbable and inappropriate features in the epic.
6. Zeus supplied with ambrosia by doves: *Odyssey* 12.62.
7. *Odyssey* 12.447.
8. *Odyssey* 22.
9. An obscure phrase, probably suggesting that, Homer being Zeus of poets (cf. Quintilian 10.1.46), he sometimes dozes and dreams (*bonus dormitat Homerus*, Horace, *Ars Poetica* 359).

ERICH AUERBACH ON HOMERIC STYLE

The excursus upon the origin of Odysseus' scar is not basically different from the many passages in which a newly introduced character, or even a newly appearing object or implement, though it be in the thick of a battle, is described as to its nature and origin; or in which, upon the appearance of a god, we are told where he last was, what he was doing there, and by what road he reached the scene; indeed, even the Homeric epithets seem to be in the final analysis to be traceable to the same need for an externalization of phenomena in terms perceptible to the senses. Here is the scar, which comes up in the course of the narrative; and Homer's feeling simply will not permit him to see it appear out of the darkness of an unilluminated past; it must be set in full light, and with it a portion of the hero's boyhood—just as, in the *Iliad*, when the first ship is already burning and the Myrmidons finally arm that they may hasten to help, there is still time not only for the wonderful simile of the wolf, not only for the order of the Myrmidon host, but also for a detailed account of the ancestry of several subordinate leaders (16,vv.155ff.). To be sure, the aesthetic effect thus produced was soon noticed and thereafter consciously sought; but the more original cause must have lain in the basic impulse of the Homeric style: to represent phenomena in a fully externalized form, visible and palpable in all their parts, and completely fixed in their spatial and temporal relations. Nor do psychological processes receive any other treatment: here too nothing must remain hidden and unexpressed. With the utmost fullness, with an orderliness which even passion does not disturb, Homer's personages vent their inmost hearts in speech; what they do not say to others, they speak in their own minds, so that the reader is informed of it. Much that is terrible takes place in the Homeric poems, but it seldom takes place wordlessly: Polyphemus talks to Odysseus; Odysseus talks to the suitors when he begins to kill them; Hector and Achilles talk at length, before battle and after; and no speech is so filled with anger or scorn that the particles which express logical grammatical connections are lacking or out of place. This last observation is true, of course, not only in speeches but of the presentation in general. The separate elements of a phenomenon are most clearly placed in relation to one another; a large number of conjunctions, adverbs, particles, and other syntactical tools, all clearly circumscribed and delicately differentiated in meaning, delimit persons, things, and portions of incidents in respect to one another, and at the same time bring them together in a continuous and ever flexible connection; like the separate phenomena themselves, their relationships—their temporal, local, casual, final, consecutive, comparative, concessive, antithetical, and conditional limitations—are brought to light in perfect fullness; so that a continuous rhythmic procession of phenomena passes by, and never is there a form left fragmentary or half-illuminated, never a lacuna, never a gap, never a glimpse of unplumbed depths.

And this procession of phenomena takes place in the foreground—that is, in a local and temporal present which is absolute. One might thing that the many interpolations, the frequent moving back and forth, would create a sort of perspective in time and place; but the Homeric style never gives any such impression. The way in which any impression of perceptive is avoided can be clearly observed in the procedure for introducing episodes, a syntactical construction with which every reader of Homer is familiar; it is used in the passage we are considering, but can also be found in cases when the episodes are much shorter. To the word scar (v.303) there is first attached a relative clause ("which once long ago a boar ..."), which enlarges into a voluminous syntactical parenthesis; into this an independent sentence unexpectedly intrudes (v.396: "A god himself gave him ..."), which quietly disentangles itself from syntactical subordination, until, with verse 399, an equally free syntactical treatment of the new content begins a new present which continues unchallenged until, with verse 467 ("The old woman now touched it ..."), the scene which had been broken off is resumed. To be sure, in the case of such long episodes as the one we are considering, a purely syntactical connection with the principal theme would hardly have been possible; but a connection with it through perspective would have been all the easier had the content been arranged with that end in view; if, that is, the entire story of the scar had been presented as a recollection which awakens in Odysseus' mind at this particular moment. It would have been perfectly easy to do; the story of the scar had only to be inserted two verses earlier, at the first mention of the word scar, where the motifs "Odysseus" and "recollection" were already at hand. But any such subjectivistic-perspectivistic procedure, creating a foreground and background, resulting in the present lying open to the depths of the past, is entirely foreign to the Homeric style; the Homeric style knows only a foreground, only a uniformly illuminated, uniformly objective present. And so the excursus does not begin until two lines later, when Euryclea has discovered the scar—the possibility for a perspectivistic connection no longer exists, and the story of the would becomes an independent and exclusive present.

(...)

The Homeric poems, then, though their intellectual, linguistic, and above all syntactical culture appears to be so much more highly developed, are yet comparatively simple in their picture of human beings; and no less so in their relation to the real life which they describe in general. Delight in physical existence is everything to them, and their highest aim is to make that delight perceptible to us. Between battles and passions, adventures and perils, they show us hunts, banquets, palaces and shepherds' cots, athletic contests and washing days—in order that we may see the heroes in their ordinary life, and seeing them so, may take pleasure in their manner of enjoying their savory present, a present which sends strong roots down into social usages, landscape, and daily life. And thus they bewitch us and ingratiate themselves to us until we live with them in the reality of their lives; so long as we are reading or hearing the poems, it does not matter whether we know that all this is only legend, "make-believe." The oft-repeated reproach that Homer is a liar takes nothing from his effectiveness, he does not need to base his story on historical reality, his reality is powerful enough in itself; it ensnares us, weaving its web around us, and that suffices him. And this "real" world into which we are lured exists for itself, contains nothing but itself; the Homeric poems conceal nothing, they contain no teaching and no secret second meaning. Homer can be analyzed, as we have essayed to do here, but he cannot be interpreted. Later allegorizing trends have tried their arts of interpretation upon him, but to no avail. He resists such treatment; the interpretations are forced and foreign, they do not crystallize into a unified doctrine. The general considerations which occasionally occur (in our episode, for example, v.360: that in misfortune men age quickly) reveal a calm acceptance of the basic facts of human existence, but with no compulsion to brood over them, still less any passionate impulse either to rebel against them or to embrace them in an ecstasy of submission.

MILMAN PARRY ON FORMULARY DICTION

There is only one way by which we can determine with some degree of precision which part of Homer's diction must be formulary: namely, a thorough understanding of the fact that this decision, in so far as it is made up of formulae, is entirely due to the influence of the metre. We know that the non-Ionic element in Homer can be explained only by the influence of the hexameter; in just the same way, formulary diction, of which the non-Ionic element is one part, was created by the desire of bards to have ready to hand words and expressions which could be easily put into heroic verse. The epic poets fashioned and preserved in the course of generations a complex technique for formulae, a technique designed in its smallest details for the twofold purpose of expressing ideas appropriate to epic in a suitable manner, and of attenuating the difficulties of versification.

While this diction by formulae is in itself so complicated, as we shall soon have occasion to see, that its analysis requires immense labour, its principle is none the less essentially a simple one, and can be expressed in a few words. To create a diction adapted to the needs of versification, the bards found and kept expressions which could be used in a variety of sentences, either as they stood or with slight modifications, and which occupied fixed places in the hexameter line. These expressions are of different metrical length according to the ideas they are made to express; that is, according to the nature of the words necessary for the expression of these ideas. Of these formulae, the most common fill the space between the bucolic diaeresis and the end of the line, between the penthemimeral caesura, the caesura κατὰ τρίτον τροχαῖον, or the hepthemimeral caesura and the end of the line, or between the beginning of the line and these caesurae; or else they fill an entire line. The ways in which these expressions are joined to each other so as both to make a sentence and to fill out the hexameter, are many and vary in accordance with each type of expression.

(...)

We have limited ourselves hitherto to the use of the general term *expression*. Before we decided how far we are justified in referring to the tradition such expressions as those above, before, that is, we determine the method of research proper to the study of the traditional element in Homeric diction, we must first agree on the sense on the word *formula*. In the diction of bardic poetry, the formula can be defined as an expression regularly used, under the same metrical conditions, to express an essential idea. What is essential in an idea is what remains after all stylistic superfluity has been taken from it. Thus the essential idea of the words ἦμος δ' ἠριγένεια φάνη ῥοδοδάκτυλος Ἠώς is 'when the day broke'; that of βῆ δ' ἴμεν is 'he went'; that of τὸν δ' αὖτε προσέειπε 'said to him'; and, as we shall have occasion to see in detail further on, that of πολύτλας δῖος Ὀδυσσεύς is 'Odysseus'. We can say that an expression is used regularly when the poet avails himself of it habitually, and without fear of being reproached for doing so too often. If, for example, Homer invariably uses τὸν δ' ἠμείβετ' ἔπειτα whenever he wants to express, in words that fill the line up to the feminine caesura and end in a short vowel, the idea of the predicate of a sentence whose essential meaning is 'X answered him', then these words can be considered a formula; for the frequency of the expression and the fact that it is never replaced by another prove that the poet never hesitated to use it, wherever he could, to express his thought. And again, if it turns out that Homer constantly uses a certain group of words, πολύτλας δῖος Ὀδυσσεύς for example, to express the subject of this sentence, then this group of words can be considered a formula. And if, finally, we find that the subject of τὸν δ' ἠμείβετ' ἔπειτα is generally provided by a series of expressions analogous to πολύτλας δῖος Ὀδυσσεύς, in that each of them is made up of a noun and of one or two epithetic words, we can then conclude that we are in the presence of a *formula type*. By definition and by necessity, therefore, the formula and the formula type are part of the technique which Homer used to express his ideas in his poems. But the definition in no way implies, and should in no way imply whether the formula belongs to the tradition or whether it is, on the contrary, the poet's creation. For the Homeric formula is being considered here as a means of versification, and not in terms of its traditional or original character. It is an expression which, whatever may have been its history, made the process of versification easier for the poet or poets of the *Iliad* and the *Odyssey* at the moment when these poems were composed.

(…)

But the greatest advantage in selecting the epithet as the object of our researches into traditional style is the semantic distinction which we are thereby enabled, or better, which we are thereby forced to make between two kinds of epithets—the particularized epithet, which concerns the immediate action, and the ornamental epithet, which has no relation to the ideas expressed by the words of either the sentence or the whole passage in which it occurs. And this semantic distinction leads us to a surer judgment of the traditional character of Homeric style as a whole than we can derive from the proof provided by the system. The reason for this is, that as we are forced to recognize the character of the fixed epithet in Homer, a character that distinguishes it from any epithet occurring in the work of a poet who uses an individual style, we find ourselves at grips with a conception of style entirely new to us. We are compelled to create an aesthetics of traditional style.

The matter at stake is the poet's freedom of choice. Was Homer, or was he not, obliged to use traditional formulae? And is he a greater poet for having used them, or for having rejected them and sought instead words appropriate to the particular nuance of his thought?

The conclusions of those who have demonstrated that the variety of forms observed in epic language could be explained by necessities of versification have already given rise to the objection that this would deprive the poet of all power of choice. A complicating factor is that words and forms borrowed from alien dialects are among the principal means of ennobling the style of Greek poetry. Thus E. Drerup protests that to make the exigency of verse alone responsible for the non-Ionic elements in Homeric language is to exclude from the problem 'that subjective element which in all poetry, without exception, determines the formation of language and verse: I mean, the art of the poet....' He goes on to add that if the poet uses such forms as τάων, πάντεσσι, ἄμμες, it is not because he had to: he could perfectly well have used the Ionic form of these words, if in a different part of the line. According to Drerup, he chose Aeolic forms because he judged their tone more suitable for his poetry as well as because they were more manageable in versification.[1]

But here Drerup is wrong and K. Witte is right: the former's reasoning is based on a fundamental error: one cannot speak of the poet's freedom to choose his words and forms, if the desire to make this choice does not exist. Homer had inherited from his predecessors a language whose several elements were used solely in accordance with the needs of composition in hexameters. If it had been otherwise, if this or that archaic or Aeolic word or form had survived chiefly because it was able to give the style the nobility of a λέξις ξενική, then the system of epic language would have included a multitude of metrically equivalent elements. But this is not the case. Generally speaking, whenever Homer has to express the same idea under the same metrical conditions, he has recourse to the same words or the same groups of words. Where Witte is at fault is in not having confined himself to showing that the non-Ionic elements in epic language, at the moment when they became alien to the spoken language of the bards and of their audience, received an artistic consecration, and that this was what *maintained* them in heroic language. It does indeed give a false impression of the character of this language to imply that its creation was, so to speak a mechanical process. This is a mistake which we shall be at pains to avoid in these pages, when we come to deal with the origin and development of formulary diction. None the less, Witte expressed no more than the truth when he said that in Homer, convenience of versification alone, determines the choice of a dialectal or artificial element in the traditional language. Homer's use of this or that archaic or dialectal form is a matter of habit and convenience, not of poetic sentiment.

Note

1. *Homerische Poetik*, 121 ff.

SIMON GOLDHILL ON THE PROEM OF THE *ODYSSEY*

῎ΑΝΔΡΑ: What is (to be) recognized in this first word of the *Odyssey*? The first question I wish to raise is how exemplary, how generalizable, a (male, adult) figure the subject of this epic is presented to be—a question focused in an English translation by the difficulty of choosing between 'a man', 'the man' or even 'man'. For the uneasy tension between paradigmatic model and unique individual typical of the representation of heroes is especially marked in the case of Odysseus. On the one hand, recent critics have emphasized how Odysseus' reintegration is 'a return to humanity in the broadest sense'[1]—a paradigmatic representation of (a) man's reaffirmation of social identity. The boundaries and values of the *oikos* (household) are mapped by the transitions and transgressions of Odysseus' journey: Odysseus' travels leave behind both the extremes of civilization experienced among the Phaeacians, and also the extremes of violent transgression and distorted versions of human culture experienced in the non-human encounters leading to the Phaeacians, as the hero struggles to regain the *oikos*, disordered by his absence. Human social existence and man's place in it become defined through these different views of alternative or corrupted order. So, the normative thrust of the *Odyssey* is to be discovered not merely in the punishment of the suitors' wrongdoing but also in the projection and promotion of the norms of culture—an articulation of man's place. (And particularly since Vidal-Naquet's classic analysis of land, agriculture, food and

119

sacrifice, many other aspects of this patterning of norm and transgression have been outlined—from the fundamental social institutions of marriage and guest-friendship to such diverse signs of the cultural system as trees, dogs, weaving, bathing …)[2] In *andra*, then, there is to be recognized a paradigmatic and normative representation of what it is to be a man in society, an announcement that the narrative to come will explore the terms in which an adult male's place is to be determined.

On the other hand, Odysseus is not an allegorical figure like Everyman. He is also *the* man whose special qualities allow him to survive a unique set of wanderings and sufferings and to make his return to a particular position. So, indeed, *andra* is immediately qualified by its (first and marked) epithet *polutropon*, 'of many turns'. Since antiquity, the ambiguity of this term has been debated.[3] As Pucci has analysed at greatest length, *polutropos* is the first of a series of distinctive *polu*-epithets indicating Odysseus' 'chief characteristic: versatility, resources, tricks, stories …'[4] (So the proem goes on to emphasize Odysseus' 'many [*polla*] wanderings' (1) to see towns of 'many [*pollon*] men' (2), and to suffer 'many [poll'] pains', (3) *Polutropos*, 'of many turns', implies both 'of many wiles' and 'of many journeys', and the ambiguity is significant in that it is Odysseus' wily turns of mind that allow him to survive his wanderings: the many experiences of Odysseus and his quality of being *polutropos* are linked by more than the repetition of *pol-*. What's more, Pucci adds a third meaning, 'of many turns of speech', derived from *tropos* in its sense 'figure of speech', 'trope'—although there is no secure evidence for this sense of *tropos* before the fifth century. What can be said, however, is that it is a defining aspect of Odysseus' wiliness that he is the master of tricky language (and Hermes, the only other figure called *polutropos* in the Homeric corpus, is the divinity associated particularly with deceitful communication and the problems of exchange[5]). So, too, that Odysseus is the *object* of a multiplicity of (rhetorical) descriptions in the epic is an integral element not only of the many-sided representation of the hero, but also, more specifically, of the instantiation of his *kleos*, his renown— 'to be talked of by many' ('Tell me, Muse….') There is, then, to be recognized in *andra*, especially as it begins its lengthy glossing with the specific and polyvalent *polutropos*, the sign of a particular figure—'the (especial, inimitable, famous) man'.

As Odysseus struggles to reinstitute the norms of the *oikos*, and proves the only man capable of winning the struggle, this ambivalent paradigmatic status informs the narrative of *nostos* (return). And *andra* is programmatic of this.

The surprising lack of a proper name in the first line(s) of the epic, then, prompts the question not simply of *to whom* does the opening expression refer, but of *what* is (to be) recognized in such a periphrastic reference.[6] Indeed, the withholding of the name invests the proem with the structure of a *griphos*, a riddle, an enigma, where a series of expressions (of which *polutropon* is the first) successively qualifies the term *andra* as the name 'Odysseus' is approached. The rhetorical strategy of the gradual revealing (that is also a continuing (re)defining) provides a programmatic model for the narrative of Odysseus' gradual re-establishment on Ithaca, where each encounter successively and cumulatively formulates the character and *kleos*, 'renown', of the hero, as his recognition is approached.

This nameless opening expression, however, does not merely set up the mapping of *andra* (as man, adult, male, husband ...) but also poses the question of what is at stake in a (proper) name, of what is the difference between saying *andra* and saying 'Odysseus': from the Cyclops' cave to standing in the hall before the suitors, speaking out the name of Odysseus is replete with significance. *Andra*, then, also announces the concealment and revealing of the name that plays a crucial role in the *kleos* of Odysseus' return. Yet, as Pucci also notes, the name is displaced by an adjective, *polutropon*, that itself expresses the very quality of deceptive wiliness that is seen most strikingly in Odysseus' constant disguises, which, precisely, withhold the proper name.[7] *Polutropon*, in other words both marks Odysseus' capability to manipulate language's power to conceal and reveal, and, at the same time, *enacts* such a revealing and concealing. There is to be recognized here, then—another programmatic gesture—how the *Odyssey* in a self-reflexive way highlights, first, words and their use as a concern.

There is, then, in these first words a multiform programmatic expression. The question of what is (to be) recognized in the first word(s) of the *Odyssey* is itself framed to emphasize how, in responding to this narrative which progresses through a series of defining recognitions, the reader or audience is necessarily implicated in a process of drawing out significances, connotations, relations between words (phrases, lines, scenes)—inevitably implicated, that is, in a process of defining and recognition. (And in Greek *anagignôskein* means both 'to read and 'to recognize'.)⁸ There is, then, also to be recognized in the first words of the *Odyssey* the (self-) involvement of the reader or audience in comprehending the narrative of recognition—which, as we will see, is fundamental to the normative project of the *Odyssey*.

Notes

1. Segal (1962) 20. The paradigmatic qualities of Odysseus are also discussed by Taylor (1961); Segal (1967); Vidal-Naquet (1981(1970)), Austin (1975) 81–238; Foley (1978); Niles (1978); Goldhill (1984); 183ff; Rutherford (1985)

2. On marriage, see Hatzantonis (1974); Pomeroy (1975) 16–31: Gross (1976); foley (1978); Forsyth (1979); Northrup (1980); Goldhill (1984) 184–95; Goldhill (1986a) 147–51; on guest friendship, Finley (1954) 109–14; Gunn (1971); Stagakis (1975) 94–112; Stewart (1976); Edwards (1975); Bader (1976); Kearns (1982); Herman (1987); and Murnaghan (1987) 91–117, who rightly relates this institution to the problem of recognition; on trees, see Finley (1978) 78–9 who writes 168: 'Trees progressively mark his [Odysseus'] return.' On the olive, see Segal (1962) 45, 55 (with n.31 and n.41). Vidal–Naquet (1981(1970) 60–61 notes that the tree under which Odysseus shelters on the beach at Scheria (as Odysseus returns from the wild travels to the civilized world of the Phaeacians) is half wild, half domestic olive! On dogs, Rose, G. (1979); Goldhill (1988c) 9–19 (both with further bibliography); on weaving Snyder (1981); Jenkins (1985); Goldhill (1988c) 1–9; Segal (1967) 337–9; on bathing, Segal (1967) 329–34.

3. For modern discussion specifically on *polutropon*, see in particular Rüter (1969) 34–9; Detienne and Vernant (1978) 27–54, especially 39–43: Pucci (1982); Clay (1983) 29ff. See also Basset (1923); van Groningen (1946). Millman Parry singles out the word as his first example of a particularized epithet (1971)154. Bekker (1863) inaugurates a lengthy discussion among Analytic scholars, for which Rüter has extensive bibliography. For ancient discussion, see, e.g. Porphyr. Schol. ad *Od*. I.I. = Antisthenes fr. 51 Decleva Caizzi. At Plato *Hipp. Min.* 365c–d, Hippias, in discussing Homer, joins

πολύτροπον 'of many turns', and ψευδῆ,'lying', as apparent synonyms, but Socrates says he will not discuss Homer since one cannot ask what he had in mind when he composed the lines. For the most interesting modernist treatment of *polutropos*, see Ellman (1982).

4. Pucci (1982) 51.

5. The only other example in the *Odyssey* is *Od* 10.330 where Odysseus is recognized by Circe form an oracle as he tricks her. It occurs elsewhere in the Homeric corpus only in the *Hymn to Hermes* 13 and 439, applied to Hermes, for whose tricky qualities, see Kahn (1978). Hermes also helps Odysseus with Circe in particular (*Od.* 10.277ff) and supports Odysseus' grandfather, Autolycus (*Od.* 19.397ff).

6. The lack of name has often been commented on. The modern Analytic debate begins with Bekker (1863) (see n. 3). Wilamowitz in a fine example of Analytic rhetoric regards it as a 'carelessness' (Unbedachtsamkeit) that the poet 'forgets to name the man of many turns' ('*den* ἀνηρ πολύτροπος *zu nennen vergisst*' (1884) 16. For an extensive bibliography, see Rüter (1969) 34–52 to which can be added the important works of Dimock (1956); Austin (1972); Clay (1976); Clay (1983) 10–34.

7. Pucci (1982) 49–57.

8. Although *anagignôskein* is a Homeric term, there is depicted, of course, no scene of 'reading' in a narrow sense. There are, however, innumerable scenes that revolve around the difficulties of interpretation and communication. Hence my phrase 'reader or audience': it is used to avoid two chimaeras of Homeric criticism: the speculative reconstruction of necessary restrictions for the audience's comprehension of an oral performance; the presupposition that an oral performance necessarily requires clarity, transparency or ease of comprehension. For the implications of such a privileging of the spoken word, see the famous discussion of Derrida (1976), well used specifically for Homer by Lynn-George (1988).

PIERRE VIDAL-NAQUET ON ODYSSEUS' RETURN TO HUMANITY

For Odysseus to leave this fantasy world means to leave a world that is not the world of men, a world which is by turns super-human and sub-human, a world in which he is offered divinity by Calypso but also threatened by Circe with reduction to the condition of an animal. And he must leave it to return to the world of normality. The *Odyssey* as a whole is in one sense the story of Odysseus's return to normality, of his deliberate acceptance of the human condition.

There is therefore no paradox in saying that, from the Lotus-Eaters to Calypso by way of the land of the Cyclopes and the Underworld, Odysseus meets with no creature which is strictly human. There is of course sometimes room for doubt: the Laestrygones, for example, have an agora, the mark of political life; but physically they are not as men are but giants (10.114, 120). Circe causes us to wonder whether we are dealing with a woman or a goddess: but finally, just as with Calypso, the humanity is merely in the outward form, in the voice. She is in truth, the 'terrible goddess with a human voice' (10.136; 11.8; 12.150, 449: cf.10.228). Twice Odysseus asks himself what 'eaters of bread' he has landed among—that is, what men. But in each case the point is that he is not among 'bread-eaters' but among the Lotus-Eaters and the Laestrygones (9.89; 10.101)

There follows from this a signal implication, that the 'stories' rigorously exclude anything to do with working the land, or with arable land itself insofar as it is worked. The Thrace of the Cicones is the last cultivated land Odysseus encounters: there he eats mutton and drinks wine; and there he obtains the wine he later offers the Cyclops (9.45ff., 161–5, 197–211). Euripides's Odysseus, when he lands in an unknown land, asks Silenus, 'Where are the walls and the city towers?' The answer comes: 'Stranger, this is no city. No man dwells here' (*Cyclops* 115–16). Here it is fortifications which are the symbol of the presence of civilized humanity, or indeed of humanity at all. But Homer's Odysseus looks for cultivated fields, for the sign of human labour. When the Achaens reach Circe's island, they search in vain for the *erga brotôn*, the 'works of men', that is, for crops. But all they see is scrub and forest, where stag-hunts can be organized (10.147, 150, 157–63, 197, 251). In the land of the Laestrygones, the sight of smoke might be taken as evidence of domestic hearths and the presence of human-beings (10.99). But there is 'no trace either of the work of oxen or the work of men' (10.98). The Sirens live in a meadow, as do the gods elsewhere (12.159; cf. *Homeric Hymn to Hermes* 72; Euripides, *Hippolytus* (73–4). Although Calypso's island is wooded and even possesses a vine, this is never said to be cultivated (5.63–74).

There is one specifically human tree present in the world of the 'stories': the olive, the tree of whose wood Odysseus built his bed, the fixed point of his home (23.183–204). And in fact the olive is on a number of occasions the means of Odysseus's escape from danger, in several different forms. It provides the stake with which he bores through the Cyclops's eye; and the handle of the axe with which he builds his boat (9.219–20; 5.234–6;cf Segal, 1962: 45, 62, 63). And although it is true that when he is with Aeolus, Circe, or Calypso, Odysseus has plenty to eat, and that the poet playfully draws attention to the vast difference between the gods' meals and those of men (5.196–9), we are never told where it comes from or who produced it.

A second exclusion is entailed by this exclusion of cultivated land: that of the sacrificial meal, which we saw from Hesiod to be so intimately related to the first. One could almost, in a sense, extend to the entire world of the stories the remark Hermes jokingly makes to Calypso when he arrives on her island: 'Who would you choose to cross this waste of salt-water? There is not in these parts a single city of mortal men to offer rich hecatombs to the gods' (5.100–2). But only in a sense. For the sacrifice which Odysseus offers to the dead in accordance with Circe's instructions and with lambs she has provided is performed in a trench, and is intended to provide blood for the feeding of the dead (10.516–40, 571–2; 11.26–47)—it is the opposite of a sacrificial meal, whose purpose is to feed the living. And the same is true of the victims which Odysseus promises the dead and Teiresias that he will offer on his return: a barren cow and a black ram (10.521–5; 11.29–33).

In the land of the Cyclopes, Odysseus's companions offer sacrifice (9.231), as Polyphemus himself does not. But it is not a blood-sacrifice, for they are living on cheese (9.232). And the sacrifice they offer on the island just across from that of the Cyclopes—which is abnormal because the victims are the sheep belonging to Polyphemus, animals not reared by man—is rejected by Zeus (9.551–5): even when a human community does sacrifice in non-human territory, the sacrifice is improper.

This island where man and nymph dwell together, cut off from everything and everyone, alone in amorous confrontation and in a solitude made for two, is located in a sort of marginal space as a place apart, far from the gods and far from humans.[10] It is a world located elsewhere: neither that of the ever-youthful immortals (even though Kalypso is a goddess[11]), nor that of human beings subject to old age and death (even though Odysseus is a mortal man), nor that of the dead under the Earth in Hades. Odysseus has disappeared, without leaving a trace, into a sort of no-place where he lives a parenthetical existence.

Like the Sirens, Kalypso charms Odysseus—she can herself sing with a beautiful voice—as she pours forth endless litanies of sweet love: *aiei de malakoisi kai haimulioisi logoisi / thelgei.* *Thelgei:* she enchants and bewitches him so that he might forget Ithaka, *hopôs Ithakês epilêsetai.*[12]

For Odysseus, forgetting Ithaka means cutting the ties that still connect him to his life and his own people, and to those loved ones who for their part remain attached to his memory, whether they hope against hope for him to return alive or whether they are ready to erect the funerary *mnêma* for a dead Odysseus. But so long as he remains secluded and hidden with Kalypso, Odysseus' state is neither that of the living nor that of the dead. Although still alive, he is already (and ahead of time) like someone blotted out from human memory. To repeat Telemachus's words at 1.235, he alone of all men has become by will of the gods invisible, *aistos.* He has disappeared "out of sight, out of knowledge," *aistos, apustos*—beyond reach of human eye or ear. If at least, the young boy adds, he died normally, under Troy's walls or in the arms of his comrades-in-misfortune, "all the Achaians would have heaped a grave mound over him / and he would have won great fame, *mega kleos,* for himself and his son hereafter" (1.239–40). But the Harpies have carried him off: the living have nothing more to do with him, as a man belonging nowhere bereft of remembrance, he no longer has fame; vanished, obliterated, he has disappeared without glory, *akleiôs*.[13] For the hero whose ideal is to leave behind a *kleos aphthiton*, an "undying glory," could there be anything worse than disappearing this way, *akleiôs*, without glory?[14]

What then does Kalypso's seduction offer Odysseus to make him "forget" Ithaka? First of all, naturally, escape from the challenges of the return, the miseries of seafaring, and all the pains that she as a goddess knows in advance will afflict him before he finally regains his native land.[15] But these are still mere trifles. The nymph has much more to offer him: If he agrees to remain with her, she promises to make him immortal and to spare him forever from old age and death. He will live in her company as a god, immortal, in the permanent bloom of youth, for never to die and never to know the decrepitude of old age are what one stands to gain from love shared with the goddess.[16] But there is a price to pay in Kalypso's bed for this escape beyond the borders that mark the universal human condition. Sharing divine immortality in the nymph's arms would constitute for Odysseus a renunciation of his career as an epic hero. Were he no longer to figure as a model of endurance in a text that, like the *Odyssey*, sang his trials, he would have to allow his memory to be erased in the minds of humans and his posthumous fame to be taken from him; and though still alive, he would have to allow himself to sink into the depths of oblivion. Ultimately, he would have to accept an obscure, anonymous immortality—as anonymous as the death of those humans who could not take on a heroic fate and form in Hades the indistinct mass of the "nameless," the *nônumnoi*.[17]

The Kalypso episode presents, for the first time in our literary tradition, what might be called the heroic refusal of immortality. For the Greeks of the archaic period, Odysseus could not really claim as a personal achievement this eternal afterlife shared with Kalypso, since no one on earth would know of it, nor would anyone remember the name of the hero from Ithaka to celebrate it. Unlike us, Homer's Greeks could not attribute importance to the absence of death—in their eyes an absurd hope for mortals—but in a tradition based on memory, they would value the unbounded endurance among the living of a glory acquired in life, at the cost of life, throughout an existence where life and death cannot be separated.

On the shore of this isle where immortality hangs on a single word, Odysseus sits on a rock, staring at the sea, bemoaning and sobbing his lot all day long. He is melting, liquifying, into tears. His *aiôn*, or "life force," saps out of him continuously (*kateibeto aiôn*) in *pothos*, or "sorrowful regret," for his mortal life. Likewise, at the other end of the world, Penelope is for her part consuming her *aiôn* in tears of regret for the vanished Odysseus.[18] She weeps for a living man who is perhaps now dead; he, on an isle of immortality that cuts him off from life as though he were dead, weeps for his existence in life as a creature destined to die.

Gripped by nostalgia for the fleeting, ephemeral world to which he belongs, our hero no longer relishes the charms of the nymph.[19] If he comes at night to sleep with her, it is because he must. He joins her in bed—she with desire, he without.[20]

It is for these reasons, then, that Odysseus rejects this immortality granted by a woman's favor; by removing him from what constitutes his life, it leads him at last to find death desirable. Gone is *erôs*, gone is *himeros*, gone is love or desire for the nymph with the lovely hair. Now, *thanein himeiretai*, "he longs to die" (1.59).

Nostos, his return; *gynê*, Penelope, his wife; Ithaka, his homeland, son, aging father, faithful companions; and then *thanein*, to die. These are all those things toward which Odysseus' power to love, his nostalgic desire, and his *pothos* yearn because he has wearied of Kalypso and has refused a non-death that is also a non-life. His is a yearning for life, precarious and mortal; for trials; for wanderings renewed time and again without end; and for a fate of heroic endurance which he must accept in order to become himself, Odysseus. For this is Odysseus of Ithaka, whose name the text of the *Odyssey* still sings today as it recounts his returns and celebrates his undying glory. But of this man the poet would not have had a word to say—and we not a word to hear—had he remained far from his own people, immortal, and "hidden" with Kalypso.[21]

Notes

10. For the "faraway" nature of the island, cf. *Od.* 5.55; far away from the gods: 5.80 and 100; far away from humans: 5.101–2.

11. The nymph is on several occasions called *thea* or *theos*, "goddess" (1.14 and 51; 5.78; 7.255; esp. 5.79, where the two *theoi* are the pair Kalypso-Hermes; 5.118, where Kalypso includes herself in the group of goddesses who have fallen in love with a mortal; 5.138, where before yielding she grants that no [other] *god* can oppose the will of Zeus; 5.192–94, where the pair Kalypso-Odysseus refers to a *god* and a man, *theos* and *anêr*).

12. *Od.* 5.61 and 1.56–57 (repeated in book 5).

13. *Od.* 1.241.

14. Cf. J-P. Vernant, "La Belle Mort et le cadaver outragé," in *La Mort, les morts dans les sociétés anciennes*, ed. G. Gnoli and J.-P. Vernant (Cambridge and Paris, 1982); 45–76.

15. *Od.* 5.205ff.

16. *Od.* 5.136; 209; 7.257; 8.453; 23.336.

17. Hesiod, *Works and Days* 154. In the context of archaic Greek culture, where the category of the individual is very different from the "ego" of today, only the posthumous glory of death can be called "personal." The immortality of an "invisible and unknown" beng remains outside of what for the Greeks constitutes a subject's individuality—i.e., essentially his renown; cf. J.-P. Vernant, "La Belle Mort" (above, note 14), 12 and 53.

18. Odysseus' tears: *Od.* 1.55; 5.82–83, 151–53, and 160–61; Penelope's tears: 19.204–09; 262–65.

19. *Od.* 5.153: Odysseus' vitality is drained out in tears "since the nymph was no longer pleasing to him," *epei ouketi hêndane nymphê*.

20. At night Odysseus goes back to Kalypso of necessity, *anankê*; against his wishes because she wishes it: 5.154–55.

21. It is proverbial that, once an exploit has been accomplished, it must not remain hidden (*kalypsai*) in silence. What is needed is the divine melody of praise poetry (Pindar, *Nemean* 9.6–7).

JEAN STAROBINSKI ON THE INSIDE AND THE OUTSIDE

The complete mastery of self, the perfect modulation of relationships with enemies and friends find their embodiment in Ulysses. As skilful at talking as at fighting, full of ingenious ruses, he mans the barrier of the teeth, safeguarding his soul and his words. When the occasion warrants it, he can employ wile to hide his violent intentions; above all, he is capable of repressing his anger, of calculating the right moment to strike.

He therefore has at his disposal many means of action: *polymechanos* (whose approximate translation is "careful," "having a thousand resources") is one of his epithets. If he figures, in homiletic tradition, as the rational hero *par excellence*, that is so because he always knows how to choose, from among the resources that assure him mastery of speech, of tongue-minding and of fabulation, the one most appropriate to the occasion; simulation, dissimulation, candor, entreaties. The virtuosity with which he governs his words—now hiding his thought, now containing passion—qualifies him to brave the harshest outside. Whatever adventures and voyages the poet fancies, Ulysses' multiple powers prove equal to the multiplicity of his trials. Now his powers, on closer reflection, will be seen to consist, for the most part, in the act of discriminating at every turn between what one must store (inside, in the secret of the heart, in the breast) and what it is meet to surrender: concealing or openly admitting his desire to return, using an alias or his true name, inventing a past or giving a faithful account of events. Ulysses' mastery derives from his ability to appraise, while moving through an almost ubiquitously hostile world, the exact portion of himself that can be externalized: danger is everywhere so proximate, that one is safest without a handle for others to grasp—as No Man. And to test the intentions of other people, one is well advised to approach them in borrowed guise. Abetting this strategy of prudence, Athena changes her protégé's appearances, even though, on at least one occasion, she is repaid in kind when Ulysses, failing to recognize her, relates a story made from whole cloth and speaks to her "contrary to the truth" (*Odyssey*, XIII, 250–331). It is therefore the danger everywhere present in foreign lands that provokes the will to sunder *outside* from inside, what *can* be said from what *must* be kept secret. At times prudence counsels against absorbing that which originates *outside*. Ulysses drinks Circe's philtre, but only after making it anodine with "the herb of life." The hero has a greater capacity than ordinary men for letting dangerous substances enter him because he knows which antidotes to take, or else because a god reveals them to him. Here again we see acquired mastery at work determining what may cross "the barrier of the teeth" or of the ears. Our interest in the hero grows keener when the narrator shows him more completely exposed to the outside, more apparently *open* to external danger, but also more ingenious, his wit at the ready.

(...)

The end of *The Odyssey* brings home this considerable lesson: it is outside, through the mediation of exteriority, that the hidden part, the dissimulated identity, can become manifest. To be sure, the beggar, at Eumaeus' house and with Athena's assistance, suddenly acquires a godlike countenance and, to the son who wants to welcome him as a god, Ulysses need say only, "I am thy father" (*Odyssey*, XVI, 188). In the palace, however, decisive *signs* must be adduced, palpable signs: the strength it takes to draw a bow, for example. But this sign is merely an index of strength—it doesn't prove the strength to be Ulysses', it doesn't guarantee *sameness*, vouchsafe identity, or establish beyond doubt a bond with the past. If Argos recognizes his master instinctively, the recognition is muffled inside animal excitement and comes to naught when the dog dies. Irrefutable proof, when given, will be furnished by lasting traces of past acts: traces branded in the body, traces graven into places and objects.

The "great scar": this "true sign" (*Sema ariphrades, Odyssey,* XXXI, 217) results from an old encounter with animal violence, with the boar's tusk. Identity, which deep-seated conviction no longer suffices to guarantee after twenty years' absence, is sealed by an external mark, the vestige of a "long gash in the flesh" (XIX, 450). For Penelope, however, Ulysses will not have done proving his titles until, goaded to it by a ruse, he relates the manner in which he himself built their conjugal bed:

> So she spoke, and made trial of her husband. But Ulysses, in a burst of anger, spoke to his true-hearted wife, and said: "Woman, truly this is a bitter word that thou hast spoken. Who has set my bed elsewhere?

Hard would it be for one, though never so skilled, unless a god himself should come and easily by his will set it in another place. But of men there is no mortal that lives, be he ever so young and strong, who could easily pry it from its place, for a great token is wrought in the fashioned bed, and it was I that built it and none other. A bush of long-leafed olive was growing within the court, strong and vigorous, and in girth it was like a pillar. Round about this I built my chamber, till I had finished it, with close-set stones, and I roofed it over well, and added to it jointed doors, closefitting. Thereafter I cut away the leafy branches of the long-leafed olive, and trimming the trunk from the root, I smoothed it around with the adze well and cunningly, and made it straight to the line, thus fashioning the bed-post; and I bored it all with the augur. Beginning with this I hewed out my bed, till I had finished it, inlaying it with gold and sliver and ivory, and I stretched on it a thong of ox-hide, bright with purple. Thus do I declare to thee this token; but I know not, woman, whether my bedstead is still fast in its place, or whether by now some man has cut from beneath the olive stump, and set the bedstead elsewhere."

So he spoke, and her knees were loosened where she sat, and her heart melted, as she knew the sure tokens which Ulysses told her. (XXIII, 181–206)

The word *sema*, "sign" or "token," reappears in this episode four times (XXIII, 188; 202; 206; 225): "a great token is wrought (*tetuktai*) in the fashioned bed (*en lechei asketo*)"—this would be the literal translation of verses 188–189. This token is known only to the spouses (and to a faithful domestic). It belongs to a private "code" used by the couple whose mutual recognition it assures. This, it is the permanence of the possession of the "code" that insures the permanence of Ulysses' identity. But what "significant," in the theological sense, is involved here?—an artifact wrought in former days by Ulysses with his own hands, unaided. Ulysses' words, describing the construction of a place and an object, have as *bona fides*, the durable object, the bed, which, in the capacity of immutable "referent" Homer attributes to it, carries more evidential weight than the articulation of deep-seated certitude. The "I have made," together with the object made, are more probative than the "I am" would have been. Outside, in the room and bed he hewed, lies the proof of Ulysses' personal being, *confirmation* of his true essence.

Erich Auerbach, addressing himself to the Homeric epic, laid special emphasis upon the beautiful, flat exteriority of the narrative development: "... externalized, uniformly illuminated phenomena, at a definite time and in a definite place, connected together without lacunae in a perpetual foreground..."[9] In regard to the passage we are reading, one need add only this: the narration of external activity stands *in place of* (in the fullest sense of that term: it develops in space, it establishes itself in space) the expression of internal identity. This narration adduces the sufficient equivalent of it, for it proves sufficient to allay Penelope's lingering doubt. The individual having produced such strong marks outside, his *being* is effectively fulfilled therein and need not seek itself elsewhere.

No need to allegorize; it is quite enough to read the text, giving each term its full weight. In this case, our interpretation does not set out in quest of a hidden message; right before it, it has the *bare* account in which—from Penelope's viewpoint—the last shadow of Ulysses' incognito fades away. For the reader (or listener) who never doubted Ulysses' identity, it is—like the story of the wound and the scar—only one more hitherto unknown fragment of the past coming to light: everything stands revealed. What Ulysses must tell (and this represents his last trial) is the singular way in which he built the conjugal bed. His Return will then be "for good," the end clasping the beginning. Title to legitimate property, in the absence of written acts (of which Homeric literature is ignorant) inheres in the shared secret of that intimate labor through which room and bed came to be. "Deep-seated" identity therefore reveals itself through that sovereign means of exteriorization which is the laborious act, and the narrative recalling (still another exteriorization) of this old act abolishes the last obstacle to return; it assures the hero's reconquest of his plenipotentiary rights. Hegel is not our authority here, but the words and images themselves, the way they follow one another in the clear evidence of the Homeric epos.

If proofs of identity are conveyed in the account of an external act, let us note that the object of this external act is the construction of a material *interior*: well-joined doors, a roof that seals the nuptial chamber with "close-set stones." Ulysses fashions an enclosure within an enclosure; the image drawn here is that of a concentric structure, of a sealed place, of a protected *inside*.

The center of this place is marked by the olive tree—vertical, living at first, then transubstantiated into carved material. It sprang forth (*ephu*) majestically long before the chamber was built; its very presence incited Ulysses to undertake his construction. The tree commands the space that toil organizes round about it. It is a natural "given," invigorated by the sap that brings forth leaves in profusion and endows the trunk with great girth and solidity. Having been stripped and hewn, it goes on plunging its roots into the earth: the vegetal energy it carried inside itself is transmitted, by a kind of metonymic continuity, to the bed ensconced within its wood. The "cultural"[10] work of decoration and luxury inheres in the massive natural presence. This rich piece of handiwork was made to stay put.

Doesn't the wood of the olive tree, anchored to earth by its roots, represent "external" nature in the *thalamos*? Does it not appear to us as the pure *outside* which the "cultural" act of building holds captive in the very center of its artifice? But we can invert the terms and say with equal veracity that the earth into which the roots plunge is a living inside that fosters the tree's growth; the unshakeable bond with the soil establishes a continuity allowing the primitive vegetal power, or *physis*, to subsist within the cultural handiwork. Having preserved the trunk of the olive tree, the faithful wife thus preserved the natural sign of the center, the reshaped hole that remains as ever it was. This makes her husband's return, and a revival of their former happiness, possible.

As we have seen, the relative position of inside and outside constantly shifts. When Ulysses strips the olive tree, squares it, and bores holes with an augur, it is from the outside that his work does violence to the tree's lovely natural presence. But in this case, violence is the application of a learned skill (Ulysses works *eu kai epistamenos*), man's inner aptitude developing through mastery exercised over the object—over the external raw material. And all this, related in the past, evoked like a distant outside, becomes the very core of the present tense of recognition. Now that a kind of vertigo blurs the edge between outside and inside, the moment of embrace can arrive: Penelope encircles Ulysses' neck with her arms.

Notes

9. Erich Auerbach, *Mimesis* (Princeton University Press, 1953), p. 11.

10. In French "*culture*' signifies cultivation of the soil, or tillage, as well as intellectual culture. (*Tr.*)

FROMA I. ZEITLIN ON FIDELITY

Odysseus is likened to an art object overlaid with gold and silver by the hands of one endowed with the gifts of both Athena and Hephaistos. The description of this craftsman might well apply to Odysseus himself, specifically in the case of the bed that he himself has made, which he decorates in precisely the same way by embellishing it with gold and silver (and ivory). In identifying person with object, body with artifact, and in tracing the shift from a passive to an active role as two essential steps to a process of transfiguration, a powerful link is created that suggests a parallel between the bed and its maker, between the site and object of ownership that matches the physical figure of the one who constructed it. Others have pointed out the ways in which the construction of the entire bedchamber recapitulates and condenses the essence of Odysseus himself: the secret of a secret self that now may be revealed, the interplay between inside and outside, by which the external can now bring to light the truth of that hidden part and give proof of a dissimulated identity. And so it does, not only, as Starobinski observes, by replacing the assertion of "I am" with the active force of "I made it" but also through a set of semantic coincidences and transferrals, by which words of double meanings now coalesce into a powerful unity of reference. Let me explain.

The two key terms are *sêma* and *empedon*, each available for a *jeu de mots* at this critical moment. Penelope had first adverted to the "hidden signs that are only known to the two of us and no one else" (23.110). But it is left to Odysseus to join the two ideas of a *sêma* into one, when through the device of ring composition he first invokes its other, more literal, use as a distinguished mark (*mega sêma*) before he can claim at the end that this *sêma* of the bed is also a *sêma* of proof. And what, in fact, is the final verification, if not the query as to whether the bed is still *empedon* (23.203), that is, whether it remains still fixed in the earth? Only then is Penelope persuaded to acknowledge the bed as the *sêmata* she had required to ratify Odysseus' identity, and this, because she takes the sign as *empeda*, that is, as a solid and secure proof of who he is (23.205, 250; 24.346). In other words, the *sêma* that is *empedon* (i.e., the bed rooted in the earth) emerges as a *sêma empedon* (a valid sign). In these two junctures—the maker with his object, the words with their literal and figurative meanings—the system of reference gains a deeper coherence and closes in upon itself as securely as the chamber that "Odysseus built around the tree trunk, finished it, with close-set stones, and roofed it well over, adding the compacted doors, and fitting them closely together (23.190–94).

These are extraordinary measures, and rightly so, if we consider both the nature of the defensive system and what it aims to protect. If we return now to the beginning of this essay in which I quoted M. I. Finley on the habit in the heroic world "of translating every quality or state into some specific symbol, some concrete and material object," we might then instance the bed and its construction as a prooftext of this principle. But I believe there is more. The impulse to turn a social bond into a visible emblem and to represent the intimacy of inner feeling in external form has the power, in this case, not just to signify the stability of the marriage relationship but also to serve as the stabilizing factor itself of a quality, idea, or proposition that finally remains beyond the reach of all definitive proof. It is an attempt to master what is fundamentally an unmasterable situation.

First and foremost is the radical unknowability of the unexpressed secrets of a woman's desire. She might be pure of hands but not of heart, even if only for a brief moment, then or now. How is one to guarantee the constancy, the steadfastness, of that heart, especially under the present circumstances? The precondition, after all, that regulates the entire situation at Ithaka is the apparent freedom given to Penelope to *choose* the man for her husband whom her heart desires. If she is to choose "the best of the Achaeans," what would this title mean in designating the man she might desire? The contest of the bow, a traditional means for selecting a victorious suitor from among his rivals, might indicate that a heroic feat of physical prowess is to be the deciding factor. Yet because the poet structures his entire plot around Penelope's imagined state(s) of mind, we cannot exclude some cultural notion of feminine desire as an internalized emotion, hidden from view and maintained as a private and undivulged secret. If this is the case, how is that desire to be manifested, investigated, or controlled? Second, more substantively, is the nagging possibility of a real adulterous tryst that would simply have escaped the husband's notice. As a god, Hephaistos has the unusual advantage of Helios the Sun, the All-Seeing, as his reliable informer. He also has magical skills that can expose the errant couple and put them on potentially permanent display in the presence of eyewitnesses. This twofold scenario might be the wish fulfillment fantasy of more than one suspicious husband.

The case at Ithaka is perhaps an extreme example of the same problematic. Its more complex turns are predicated, first of all, on the figure of Penelope herself. The poem presents her in such a way as to assure us of her fidelity. At the same time, it endows her actions with sufficient ambiguity to arouse the need for interpretation, often with diametrically different results, if we chart the range of opinions that swirl around the evaluation of three especially significant moments: her decision to appear before the Suitors, the dream of the geese, and the setting up of the contest of the bow. As Suzuki observes, "unlike Odysseus, Penelope is portrayed from without, and the poet, while according her subjectivity, does not seek to represent it; he sees her through the eyes of the male characters around her— Odysseus, Telemachos, and the Suitors, and he conveys their uncertainty about her." Murnaghan goes further in outlining the dilemma. "Penelope's motives are difficult to assess," she remarks, "because the poet is generally uncommunicative about her thoughts, but not about Odysseus', leaving us to deduce her state of mind from outward gestures and speeches." She continues, "Because Penelope has been shown to be capable of duplicity, in particular through her trick with the shroud, it is not clear whether those speeches are to be taken at face value." Closely bound to these concerns is the asymmetrical quality of their knowledge. Hence, Penelope "is responding to the presence of the apparent stranger who is actually the returned Odysseus in disguise, so what seems to be a meeting of strangers is actually the reunion of husband and wife." Moreover, because Odysseus intends that she remain in this state of ignorance, his deception of her "is not the byproduct of the plot against the Suitors, but a major element in his strategy."

Athena, after all, had bidden Odysseus not to declare himself to Penelope "until you test your wife even more." The first reason given is that a premature reunion might divert him from his obligation to punish the Suitors' infractions of social rules and give away his identity too soon. But underlying the goddess's advice is the unspoken possibility that she might yet betray him (13.190–93). This apparently clever narrative strategy, which maintains suspense about her fidelity until the very end, is, more culturally speaking, based on the profound mistrust of women as exemplified, above all, in the foil story of Klytaimestra but also intimated in the two tales told by Helen and Menelaos. As Murnaghan puts it, "the *Odyssey's* unusually sympathetic portrait of the exemplary wife is placed in a wider context of suspicion towards women from which even she cannot altogether escape. Through the presentation of Penelope as an exception to the general rule, the poem self-consciously depicts the formation and authorization of a tradition of misogyny even as it places the counter-example at the center of its story." Furthermore, as often noted, every female figure in the poem, including Kalypso, Kirke, Arete, and even Nausikaa, contributes some element to the complex and composite portrait of Penelope. On the sinister side, Penelope most resembles Kirke. Does not she too have the charms to enchant men and turn them into swine, creatures who, like the Suitors, are perpetually at the mercy of their bellies? Like Kirke, she too might lure an unsuspecting man to her bed and, having persuaded him to lie in *philotês* with her, take advantage of his nakedness and even unman him. Homeric epic categorically defines a woman's role in the household as divided equally between the two poles of loom and bed (e.g., *Iliad* 1.31). Are not these the same two elements that Penelope's guile puts into play—the ruse of her web in the first instance and the trick of the bed in the second? Who then could be utterly certain from the start that her gift for duplicity against the Suitors in the matter of the loom might not this time be turned against her husband, precisely with regard to the marital bed?

CHARLES SEGAL ON THE EPISODE OF THE SIRENS

This perspective on heroic song also casts fresh light on the episode of the Sirens. They are described in the vocabulary of the bard: their song casts a spell (12.40; 12.44), like that of Phemius (1.337; cf. 11.334). This vocabulary links them with the ambiguous and seductive magic of Circe (10.291, 317). Their power depends emphatically on hearing. Their "voice" is itself a "song" (*aoidê*, 12.44, 183, 198), which is "clear-sounding" (*ligurê*, 12.44, 183) or "honey-voiced" (*meligêrus*, 12.187): hence the homoeopathic magic of the "honey-sweet wax," (*meliêdês*, as an antidote to its danger (12.49). It also brings the "joy" or "delight" associated with bardic song.[36]

The content of the Sirens' song is the epic tradition, the heroes' efforts at Troy, as well as "what passes on the wide-nurturing earth" (12.189–91). The rendering of the heroic tradition that the Sirens practice, however, is akin to the bardic song of Scheria: it shows heroic adventure as something frozen and crystallized into lifeless, static form, something dead and past, a subject for song and nothing more. For this reason, perhaps, they are the first adventure of Odysseus after Hades: "First you will come to the Sirens," Circe tells him (12.39); and they stand in close proximity to that dead world of purely retrospective heroism, where the only existence is in song. Yet when Odysseus had related his adventure among the dead—with the Siren-like "spell" and the art of a bard, to be sure (11.334, 368)—those shades were still a living part of his past, directly related to his *nostos*, or return (see 11.100 and 196).[37] What he hears in the Underworld stirs grief or arouses indignation (11.435–39, 465f.) and thus reinforces that longing for mother, father, and wife which is essential to his return (cf. 11.152–334). What the Sirens sing is remote from any experience. The magical charm of their sweet voice on the windless sea is epic *kleos* in the abstract, lovely but somehow dehumanized: hence the vagueness and generality of their form of *kleos* ("all things that arise on the most fertile earth," 12.191).

As the past of which the sirens sing has the deathly vacuity of what is long dead and without flesh (cf.12.45f.), so they themselves are characterized by motionlessness. As Odysseus and his men draw near, a windless calm forces them to take to the oars (12.167–72). These Sirens, unlike their later descendants in Greek art, do not fly[38] but "sit in their meadow" (12.45) and ask Odysseus to "stop the ship" (12.185) in order to hear their voice. They claim that no one "has ever yet passed by in black ship before hearing the honey-voiced speech from our mouths" (12.186f.). Escape from them, therefore, consists in keeping active, moving, passing by (12.47; 12.197).

Not only do the Sirens know of the exploits at Troy, but they also address Odysseus by the heroic epithet "great war-glory of the Achaeans" (12.184), the only place in the poem where he is so titled. This epithet occurs seven times in the

Iliad. The only other occurrences in the *Odyssey* are the formulaic lines by which Telemachus twice addresses the aged Nestor in book 3 (79 = 202). Well might the inexperienced youth at his first direct contact with the glories of Troy speak to the oldest of the Achaean worriers in these terms, for Nestor, more than any other Homeric character, lives in the past and has virtually his entire existence defined by his memories of the Iliadic world.

Odysseus, however, will continue his journey and effect a return to the living past and the living *kleos* that await him on Ithaca, not at Troy. He must therefore resist the blandishments of a heroic tradition that is frozen into spellbinding but lifeless song. What the Sirens know is too general and too remote to help him in his quest to recover Ithaca. To remain and listen to their song would be to yield to the seduction of a heroic tradition rendered in its most elegant, attractive, and deadly form, devoid of reality for the tasks that await this hero of *dolos*. The *Nekyia* and, in a different way, the lives of Nestor and Menelaus have shown this danger in lived example. The Sirens cast that danger of entrapment by the past specifically into the form of poetic song and the fascination it exercises. Were he to heed it, he, too, would be frozen into a sterile past, one of those rotting skeletons on the island. Thus his task is not to listen but to "pass by."

Rather than preserving fame by the remembering Muse of true epic song ("Muse," after all, is probably etymologically related to "memory"),[39] the Sirens being forgetfulness of home and loved ones (12.42f.). Pindar told how golden "Charmers" (*Kêlêdones*), akin to these Sirens, perched atop a mythical temple of Apollo at Delphi and sang so sweetly that the visitors "perished there apart from wives and children, their souls suspended by the honeyed voice" (*Paean* 8.75–79 in Snell and Maehler).[40] For Odysseus thus to perish obscurely on the rock to which the magic of the Sirens' song draws him would be to forget the return on which in fact his *kleos* rests.

In this temptation of "forgetting the return," the Sirens' magical spell has affinities not only with Circe but also with the Lotos-eaters. There too a man "forgets his return" (9.97 and

102; cf. 12.43). The victims of the Lotos, like Odysseus in book 12, have to be bound forcibly in the ship (9.99 and 12.196). The Sirens inhabit a "flowery meadow" (12.159); the Lotos is a "flowerlike food" (9.84).

The Sirens' flowery meadow, however, is characterized by a literal death and decay that are only implicit in the Lotos-eaters' temptation to forget the return. Circe describes the bones of "rotting men" near their meadow (12.46), and Odysseus warns his men of the danger in terms of dying or avoiding death ("But I shall tell you [Circe's prophecies], in order that we may die knowing them, or else avoiding death and doom we might escape," 12.156f.). That forgetting of *nostos* maybe even more intimately associated with the decay in Sirens' flowery meadow if, as Douglas Frame suggests, the root of *nostos* implies a return of consciousness (*noos*) in a "coming back" (*neomai*) from Hades. *Lêthê*, forgetting, also has associations with darkness and the obscurity of death.[41]

Epic song and the memory that it preserves, however, confer a victory over death. Its "imperishable fame," *kleos aphthiton*, is the exact antithesis of the Sirens' rot and decay. As Nagy has shown, *aphthiton*, whose root, *phthi-*, often describes the "withering" or "decay" of plant life (cf. the "imperishable vines" of the golden age fertility of Goat Island across from the Cyclopes, 9.133), has associations with the vital liquids or substances that overcome death: "From the present survey of all the Greek epic nouns (except *kleos*) which are described by *aphthito-*, we may posit a least common denominator in context: an *unfailing stream* of water, fire, semen, vegetal extract (wine). By extension, the gods representing these entities may also have the epithet *aphthito-*, as well as the things that they own or make."[42] True epic song counters the decay to which mortal things are subject with a *kleos* seen as close to the very essence of life, akin to the vital fluids that sustain human life and the natural world.

In the Siren episode, song not only is a ghostly imitation of epic but even becomes its own negation. This song brings death, not life. It does not go out over the broad earth among mortals. Those who succumb to it remain closed off from men, becalmed on a nameless sea, their bodies rotting in a flowery meadow. The Sirens known the secrets of the past, but it is a past that has no future life in the "remembering" of successive generations. Here the hero forgets his loved ones among whom his *kleos* might live on after his death (cf. 12.42f.). The epic bard, aided by the goddess of memory, makes the past live in the present and bridges the void between the sunless realm of the dead and the bright world of the living,[43] as Odysseus himself does in the *Nekyia* of books 11; the Sirens' song entraps the living in the putrefaction of their own hopelessly mortal remains.

(...)

The Sirens have the *terpsis* of the epic bard but no contact with the *kleos* through which the bard conquers death. The verb that repeatedly describes the "hearing" of their song is *akouein* (purely acoustic hearing, used eight times), never *kluein*, the social hearing of fame.[45] As their voice does not go beyond the nameless "island" (12.201) where they sit, so the "hearing" (*akouein*) of their song is entirely material, not the transcendent "imperishable *fame*" (*kleos*) that leads from death to life. As their victims succumb to the decay of their physical remains and are reduced to the rotting flesh of mere body, so a purely physical blocking of the ears as the corporeal organ of hearing suffices to defeat them. Indeed, Homer dwells concretely on the physical details of placing wax, a substance also used to preserve, in the ears (12.47f., 177).

Like Hesiod's Muses, the Sirens speak the language of "knowing" (12.189, 191; cf *Theog.* 27f., *Il.* 2.485f.), but no word of "memory" or "remembering" characterizes their song. All the basic elements of this song—its knowledge, pleasure, and "hearing"—are a perversion of true heroic song. Whoever heeds it is caught by the fatal "spell" of empty "delight" in a purely physical "hearing" that will isolate him far from the living memory of future men. Here he will rot away obscurely, his remains indistinguishable in a heap of rotting skin and bones, not the whole forms of the active figures of heroes who breathe and move in their deeds when the epic bard awakens the *klea andrôn*. Seen in this perspective, the episode of the Sirens is not just another fantastic adventure of Odysseus' wanderings. Through his characteristic form of mythic image, the traditional singer here finds poetic expression for the implicit values and poetics of epic songs and epic *kleos*.

Notes

36. So *terpomenos*, 12.52, and *terpsamenos*, 12.188; cf. 1.342, 347. For the Sirens' attributes of epic song, see Fränkel (1962) 10 and Reinhardt (1948) 60–62. See Pucci (1979) 121–32, especially 126ff., and Segal (1989) 332. On "hearing" in the Siren episode see 12.41, 48, 49, 52, 185, 187, 193, and 198.

37. See J. Finley (1978): "His [Odysseus'] curiosity might have been thought satisfied in the Underworld. But that revelation surrounded or concerned his own past and future; the Siren song has no tie with him.... He will reach home by what he learned in the Underworld; this other, complete, impersonal song ends a man's hope of wife and children.... The famous song expresses one side of a myth of which homecoming expresses the other; the two sides are not quite compatible" (130–31).

38. See Pollard (1965) 137–45. On the change from the flowery meadow of Homer to the cliffs of later painters and writers, see also Reinhardt (1948) 61.

39. For the Muse and "memory," see Lanata (1963) 3, with the references there cited; Pucci (1977) 22–24; and Detienne (1973) 13ff.

40. Athenaeus 8.36 (p. 290E), cited by Snell and Maehler (1975) fragment 52i, points out the affinity between these "charmers" and the Sirens in this "forgetting" of home and loved ones.

41. On *nostos* and the return to consciousness, see Frame (1978) chapter 3. On the semantic field of *lêthê*, see Hesiod *Theog.* 211–32 and Detienne (1973) 22–24.

42. See Nagy (1974) 244 and Nagy (1979) chapter 10.

43 See Vernant (1959) = (1974) 1:82–87, especially 87: "En faisant tomber la barrière qui sépare le present du passé, [la mémoire] jette un pont entre le mondes des vivants et cet au-delà auquel retourne tout ce qui a quitté la lumière du soliel.... Le privilege que *Mnemosune* confère à l'aède est celui d'un contact avec l'autre monde, la possibilité d'y entrer et d'en revenir librement. Le passé apparaît comme une dimension de l'au-delà" ("In removing the barrier that separates the present from the past [memory] makes a bridge between the world of the living and that world beyond to which everything that has left the light of the sun must return.... The privilege that Mnemosune confers on the singer is that of a contact with the other world, the possibility of freely entering it and freely returning from it. The past appears as a dimension of the Beyond"). See also Detienne (1973) chapter 2, especially 20ff.

144

45. *Akouein* is also the verb that Odysseus uses about "hearing" the Sirens when he relates this episode to Penelope in 23.326: "He heard the trilling voice of the Sirens."

HELENE P. FOLEY ON THE "REVERSE SIMILE" AND GENDER RELATIONS

Two surprisingly similar similes mark the first meeting of Penelope and Odysseus and their hard-won reunion. In the first (19.108–14) Odysses compares the reputation (*kleos*) of Penelope to that of a good and just king whose land and people prosper under him. Penelope replies that the gods destroyed her beauty on the day of Odysseus' departure for Troy; if he were to return her life and *kleos* would be fairer and greater. In the second (23.233–40) Odysseus is as welcome to Penelope as land to a shipwrecked sailor worn down by his battle with the surf. This simile at once recalls the situation of Odysseus as he struggles to land on Phaeacia (5.394–8). Thus both similes equate Penelope with a figure like Odysseus himself, as he has been and will be.

These two similes comparing a woman to a man form part of a group of similes of family or social relationship clustering almost exclusively around the incident in Phaeacia and the family of Odyssues as it struggles to recover peace and unity on Ithaca.[1] Many of these similes, like the two mentioned above, also evoke in the comparison an inversion of social role or a social theme with an equivalent difference of focus or point of view. Men are compared to women. In Book 8 (523–31) the weeping Odysseus is compared to a woman weeping over the body of her husband lost in war. As she mourns him enemy solders strike her shoulders and lead her off to slavery. The conqueror of Troy is identified with the most helpless of his former victims. Fathers are equated with children; Odysseus finds the land of Phaeacia as welcome as the life of a father recovered from sickness is to his children (5.394–8). Telemachus in his reunion with the swineherd Eumaeus is greeted as a loving father greets a son returned from ten years of travel; yet it is Odysseus, the real father who is present to

145

observe this embrace, who has returned from travels of considerable length(16.17–20). Telemachus and Odysseus lament at their reunion more intensely than sea-eagles robbed of their unfledged young (16.216–18). Odysseus has just regained his son; yet Homer marks the moment with an image of bereavement, of parents deprived of their young. These "reverse similes," as I shall call them, seem to suggest both a sense of identity between people in different social and sexual roles and a loss of stability, an inversion of the normal. The comparison of the joy of Penelope to that of a shipwrecked sailor has been interpreted, for example, as Homer's deliberate identification of Odysseus and his like-minded wife, or as one of a series of images of safety from the sea.[2] In this paper, however, I am interested in the larger pattern: why are there so many similes with this consistent change of perspective or reversal of social role in the comparison, and in particular, what is the meaning of the elaborate images of sexual inversion? How do these reverse-sex similes clarify the overall structure and meaning of the relations between man and wife?"[3]

The history of festival and comedy provide numerous examples of a world disrupted or inverted, then restored or renewed. Symbolic inversion of the sexes is frequently part of the process. From Aristophanes' Lysistrata to Shakespeare's Rosalind women in literature have assumed men's roles to restore and redefine the institutions of peace—marriage and the family—and to provide an avenue for corrective criticism of the status quo. In festival and comedy the marriage relation, in which the female is subordinate to the male, is used to express, reinforce, or criticize a far larger range of hierarchical social and economic relations.[4] In the *Odyssey* direct symbolic inversion of the sexes is delicately reserved for a few prominently-placed similes. Yet these similes can be interpreted as a significant part of a larger pattern of social disruption and restoration in the epic. Throughout his journey Odysseus experiences many cultures whose social order is an incomplete or inverted version of his own Ithaca, including variations on the place of women and the limits on their sexual, social, and political roles. In a similar way, voluntarily (through disguise) or involuntarily, Odysseus adopts or experiences a wide range of social roles other than his own. Penelope does not take inappropriate advantage of her opportunity to wield power in Odysseus' absence; yet to maintain his kingship she must come close as a woman can to doing so.[5]

Odysseus regains home in the wake of a disruption of normal economic, social, and ethical relations on Ithaca. Yet neither the characteristic form of social reproduction on Ithaca, nor its particular hierarchical social and sexual relations are fully resumed until, through the events of the poem, they have been re-argued, reclarified, and voluntary reaffirmed by all parties concerned. The continual play with social and sexual categories in the poem results not in social change but in a more flexible interpretation of social roles, and in a new understanding of what form of social and economic relations makes possible the continuity of culture on Ithaca. In the elaborate negotiations leading up to the recognition of Penelope and Odysseus, Homer, like Shakespeare in his middle comedies, manipulates the potential threat of social inversion which underlies the travels and the reverse-sex similes.[6] The power which Penelope has legitimately and skillfully wielded is not transferred by her to Odysseus until she has—albeit unconsciously—regained both his complete trust and power in her own domestic sphere. Homer's extensive treatment of Penelope's role in maintaining the kingship for Odysseus' return, and the length and elaboration of the recognition process between men and women throughout the poem reveal the mutual interdependence of husband and wife in the structure of Homeric society.[7]

(…)

At Ithaca the like-mindedness of Odysseus and Penelope is continually recreated through the long recognition process. Through this like-mindedness women like Arete and Penelope win from their husbands influence even in the external world of their society. The woman's consent is in both cases shown to be essential to the male's success in ruling, and it must be won with a special form of gentle, uncoercive negotiation.

Odysseus, contrary to Agamemnon's advice in the underworld or Telemachus' rough manners with his mother is consistently kind (*êpios*), not forceful to Penelope.[28] In both Phaeacia and Ithaca Homer gives the central place to Odysseus' ability to be indirect and graceful in his dealings with women. If this is not fully borne out in the case of Arete, it is with Penelope. Arete's role probably also pre-figures Penelope's in a restored Ithaca. I see no reason to assume, from Telemachus' adolescent attempts to break out from his mother's influence, that Penelope is to live the rest of her life isolated in the women's quarters.[29] Rather she will take her turn at giving gifts (see 19.309–11) and receiving visitors publicly at Odysseus' side. Like Arete she has won her husband's trust and shown her ability to settle disputes even among men.

This mode of complex and indirect negotiation for male-female relations in the poem becomes in Ithaca symbolic of an important dimension of Odysseus' kingship. Ithacan culture requires a comparable subtly established like-mindedness between the king and his domestic and agricultural subordinates like Eumaeus, Euycleia, the bard, and the herald. The apparent lack of contradiction in the poem between recovering *oikos* and state (the second mysteriously and abruptly accomplished by Athena-ex-machina) suggests that we can interpret Odysseus' elaborate recovery of his marriage and family as symbolic of a wider restoration of his kingdom on the same pattern.[30] Because the marriage is, as here, apparently used to express a larger range of hierarchical relations between "strangers" in the society, women have, not surprisingly, a correspondingly powerful and highly-valued social and ideological position in the poem.[31]

In order to evaluate fully the reverse-sex similes we must briefly return to an examination of the role of inversion in the structure of Odysseus' journey as a whole. Odysseus gains understanding of Ithaca, an ever-increasing desire for home and Penelope, and a renewed social flexibility through his experience of the incompletely human. Odyssey tests all the limits of his culture. He rejects the choice of becoming a god. He enters and returns from the world of the dead. At one moment he is nameless, without identity; at another he is already the hero of undying fame (Phaeacia). With Nausicaa he has the opportunity to relive a youthful marriage. On Ithaca he experiences before his time the indignity of poverty and old age. He explores the full range of nuances in the host-guest relationship. He visits cultures which, because of their isolation from war on their lack of need for agricultural or sexual reproduction offer him no social function he can recognize and accept. Odysseus never experiences the ultimate reversal from male to female. Yet numerous critics have commented on Odysseus' special ability to comprehend and respond to the female consciousness, on his "non-masculine" heroism and on his and Penelope's special affinity with the androgenous Athena.[32] The simile comparing Odysseus to a woman weeping over her dead husband in war (8.523.31) perhaps suggests how close Odysseus has come in the course of his travels, and in particular on Calypso's island, to the complete loss of normal social and emotional function which is the due of women enslaved in war. The earlier comparison of Penelope to an entrapped lion suggests her beleagured position in Ithaca, and thus resonates with this simile as well.[33] Once conqueror of Troy, Odysseus now understand the position of its victims; and it is as such a victim, aged, a beggar, and no longer a leader of men, that he reenters Ithaca.

On Circe's island his men flock around Odysseus like calves about their mother (10.410–415), and in recovering Odysseus they feel they have symbolically recovered Ithaca (10.416–17). Yet Odysseus is not Ithaca; and in his journey to the underworld he rediscovers how much of his identity depends not only on his own heroic and warlike powers but on mothers, fathers, sons, and wives. Ithaca, too, cannot fully reproduce itself without Odysseus. The cluster of reverse similes surrounding the return of Odysseus reinforce and clarify the nature of this interdependence of identity in his own culture. Odysseus regains his son and father by sharing action and work. Yet the key to his return is and has been Penelope. With Penelope he recreates mutual trust both verbally and through a gradual and delicate re-awakening of sexual feeling. The characteristics associated with both the male sphere—with its special relation to war as well as agriculture—and with the female sphere—weaving and maintaining the domestic environment—are each shown to be potentially unstable in one dimension. Odysseus' warlike virtues did not provide a safe return for his men, and sometimes, as with the Cyclops, they are directly responsible for their deaths; his armed presence violates the cultural balance of many peaceful islands on his journey. In contrast, he recovers Ithaca not merely through carefully meditated violence, but also through indirection and gentle persuasion. Conversely, uncontrolled female sexuality or irresponsible guardianship of the domestic environment are directly destructive to the cultural order of Ithaca. Yet I would emphasize here that Homer is not criticizing these "male" or "female" powers per se. Purely warlike qualities are appropriate at Troy. Circe's behavior is not inappropriate to a world where agriculture is automatic and foreign policy can be conducted by magic. After all, without the weapon of her sexuality Penelope could not have preserved Ithaca for Odysseus. Instead the poem argues the necessary limitation of each for a stable Ithacan culture.

Thus the *Odyssey* argues for a particular pattern of male-female relations within Ithaca. The reverse similes which frame the return of Odysseus reinforce and explore these interdependent relationships. The two famous similes comparing Penelope to an Odysseus-figure accomplish this purpose with particular subtlety. In contrast to the *Iliad*, where such reverse-sex similes cluster randomly around the relation of Patroclus and Achilles, the Odyssean similes are integral to the structural development of the poem.[34] Penelope's restraint in preserving Odysseus' kingship without usurping his power reveals the nature of her own important guardianship of the domestic sphere. During the period of tacit negotiation which takes place before their final recognition, Odysseus and Penelope recreate a mature marriage with well-defined spheres of power and a dynamic tension between two like-minded members of their sex.

Notes

1. Hermann Fraenkel, *Die Homerischen Gleichnesse* (Gottingen 1921), A. J. Podlecki, "Some Odyssean Similes," *Greece and Rome* 18 (1971) 82, and W.C. Scott, *The Oral Nature of the Homeric Simile, Mnemosyne* Suppl. 28 (1974) 123, all notice the structural position of these similes of family relation. Carroll Moulton, "Similes in the Iliad," *Hermes* 102 (1974) 390 and Podlecki note the inversion technique in the *Iliad* and *Odyssey* respectively. "Here we have the merest hint of unique feature of Odyssean similes... by which the poet reminds us of an important theme in the poem, but with a slight difference of focus or point of view" (Podlecki, 82). I was first introduced to notion of a "reverse simile" by John Finley, Jr. in 1970. None of the above interpretations attempt to explain these similes in the light of the social and sexual logic of the poem as a whole.

2. The first interpretation is common: for example, Podlecki (above, note 1), 90, and Marilyn B. Arthur, "Early Greece: The Origins of the Western Attitude Towards Women," *Arethusa* 6.1 (1973) 15. The second occurs in C.P. Segal, "The Phaecians and the Symbolism of Odysseus' Return," *Arion* 1.4 (1962) 43. Ann Amory, "The Reunion of Odysseus and Penelope," in Charles H. Tayler (ed.) *Essays on the Odyssey* (Bloomington, Indiana 1963, rep. 1969) 100–1 and Podlecki, 87, comment on how the king simile identifies Penelope and Odysseus.

3. In this paper I shall treat the *Odyssey* as a coherent text (including, for example, the disputed books 11 and 24), whether its coherence arises from its being the product in its final form of a single artistic consciousness or in some other way (for example, from its being the product of a coherent oral or cultural tradition).

Other recent work on Odyssean similes has tended to emphasize that the similes are few and carefully positioned. The content of many is unique, and thus, some argue, more probably composed for the place in which they appear although in conformity with an oral tradition. Amont those works not included above are C. M Bowra, *Tradition and Design in the Iliad* (Oxford 1930, rep. 1950), D. J. N. Lee, *The Similes of the Iliad and Odyssey Compared* (Melbourne 1964) and C. R. Beye, "Male and Female in the Homeric Poems," *Ramus*, 3.2 (1974) 87–101. G. P. Shipp, *Studies in the Language of Homer* (Cambridge 1953, 2nd ed. 1972) argues for the late date of the language of the similes.

4. The bibliography on this topic is extensive. I found particularly suggestive Natalie Z. Davis, *Society and Culture in Early Modern France* (Stanford 1975) 311, note 12 and her chapter "Women on Top," 124–151.

5. Jean-Pierre Vernant, *Mythe et Société en Grèce Ancienne* (Paris 1974) 57–81 and especially 77–81 emphasizes how real and important the power of a royal wife was in the absence of her husband. One has only to compare Clytemnestra's role in the *Agamemnon* of Aeschylus.

6. Many critics have treated the *Odyssey* as high comedy. Interestingly, women in Greek comedy (for example, in Aristophanes) are allowed to overstep domestic boundaries in a limited manner without incurring the disasters met by their counterparts in tragedy. In part this is because women in comedy act creatively to restore the damaged status quo. Even more important they remain chaste.

Penelope's suspension of time on Ithaca, to be discussed shortly, is also characteristic of the suspension or inversion of natural and social reality in festival and comedy.

7. Bernard Fenik, *Studies in the Odyssey* (*Hermes Einselschr.* 30, Wiesbaden 1974) in his otherwise excellent book does not fully bring out the important implications of this repeated type scene in the *Odyssey* for an interpretation of Penelope, See pp. 18–19 of this paper. Anne Amory (above, note 2) 116 comments that any recognition is delayed even though we might expect, based on what happens in the cases of Helen and Arete (in my interpretation of the type scene), some earlier response.

28. Agamemnon at 11.441 counsels Odysseus not to be *êpios* to Penelope.

29. Most students of the poem assume that the chaste Penelope will play a different role from that of Arete or Helen in the future. See, for example, M. Arthur (above, note 2) 18–19.

30. See Natalie Davis (above, note 4) for the widespread use of the marriage relation to symbolize other social relations. Homer's audience would perhaps have found Athena's role startling if this were not the case. Given the very limited role of the Homeric king in ordinary community affairs as opposed to war problems this does not seem as surprising as it would in another context.

31. Arthur (above, note 2) 13–14 and Finley both comment on the relation between a positive evaluation of women and the development of the nuclear family. Recent anthropological literature finds a similar positive evaluation of women in cultures, like that on Ithaca, where there is a relatively limited separation between the domestic and public spheres. See, for example, Louis Lamphere, "Strategies, Cooperation and Conflict Among Women in Domestic Groups," in Michelle Z. Rosaldo and Louise Lamphere (ed.), *Woman, Culture and Society* (Stanford 1974) 97–112. Finley does not, in my view, go far enough in examining the almost complete isolation of the ruling family on Ithaca. Odysseus apparently—perhaps simply for dramatic reasons—has no close kin.

32. See especially W. B. Stanford, *The Ulysses Theme* (Ann Arbor, Michigan 1963) on Odysseus' untypical heroism. The positive attitude toward women in the *Odyssey* has been made famous by Samuel Butler's classic *The Authoress of the Odyssey* and Robert Graves' novel *Homer's Daughter*.

33. See Podlecki (above, note 1) 86 on the possible reference to Penelope here. Segal (above, note 2) 28 interprets the Book 8 simile in terms of the contrast between Odysseus' real suffering and the Phaeacians' aesthetic distance from it.

34. Moulton (above, note 1) 391 ff.

A hero's status, although it derives from an association with the gods that may manifest itself in his ancestry or in divine support for his actions, is expressed, even constituted, through the honor he receives from other men. This is one aspect of the often-noted other-directedness of the Homeric self.[6] Homeric characters do not display the elaborate inner consciousness of characters in later classical and modern literature; rather they find their sense of self in their relations with the world outside them. Their identities are largely congruent with a social role that is determined by their valuation in others' eyes. Thus, they are sustained by the possession of outward signs of honor (mostly material possessions and social privileges) and are deeply threatened by the loss of those signs. For this reason, solitude is an especially harrowing experience; this can be seen from the first trial of Odysseus' endurance in the *Odyssey*, his journey from Calypso's island to Scheria in *Odyssey* 5 (the sole account in the Homeric epics of a character totally alone).

The intensity with which heroes feel threatened by a loss of honor lies behind the quarrel at the opening of the *Iliad*: the Achaeans find themselves without sufficient prizes to honor everyone, and neither Agamemnon nor Achilles can tolerate the suspension of honor that doing without a prize would mean. Neither can support the resulting disjunction between his merit, as he perceives it, and its outward expression; their view of the world does not allow for such a contradiction. Consequently, each takes drastic and eventually self-destructive action to eliminate that disjunction. Agamemnon insists on appropriating Achilles' prize, complaining that it would be unfitting for him alone of the Achaeans to be unhonored. Achilles responds more categorically by denying the capacity of this society that has diminished his own honor to confer honor properly. Proclaiming that he does not need the Achaeans at all, since he is honored by Zeus, he withdraws from Achaean society altogether.

Throughout the *Iliad* heroes are provoked to action by threated suspensions of their honor. Such threats come either in taunts by gloating enemies[7] or in rebukes by generals who call the honor of their subordinates into question in order to spur them on to further action.[8] In such speeches a hero's defeat or inactivity is interpreted as a sign that he can no longer claim the honor that has defined his position. These speeches generate a sense of crisis and provoke action because they question the connection between identity and evaluation implicit in an aristocratic society. This questioning is very clear when Athena goads Diomedes into fighting harder by suggesting that she is not really sure that he is the son of his father (*Il.* 5.800–813). The need to maintain their honor, of which such speeches are constant reminders, keeps heroes constantly performing the actions that honor rewards: it keeps them constantly risking their lives. The capacity of heroes to be provoked in this way is what helps make them heroic; it is no accident that the *Iliad's* greatest hero is noted for his quickness to anger.

Odysseus' distinguishing capacity for disguise marks him out as a hero of a different kind, a hero who not only endures but also embraces the obscurity that comes when either misfortunes or the challenges of rivals deprive him of the outer marks of heroic status. In Phaeacia, where he arrives without any emblem of his proper status, knows no one, and has no means of returning to his home (where his power is based), he chooses to suppress his name and to remain anonymous until he has again attained a position commensurate with that name.[9] On Ithaca, he responds to the usurpation of his home by younger and more numerous rivals by adopting the powerless persona of an old and homeless wanderer, and he remains unprovoked by the aggressive dishonor offered by his enemies.

Odysseus' willingness to undergo the humiliation involved especially in his Ithacan disguise suggests an appreciation of the inescapable forces that can prevent even the greatest hero and most privileged aristocrat from maintaining his eminent status. The history he adopts along with his disguise involves a fall from a position of prominence and prosperity through misfortune, and in that persona he speaks eloquently of the subjectedness of all humans to fortune and the necessity for endurance (most notably in his famous warning to Amphinomus, *Od.* 18.125–150).

But while Odysseus' disguise testifies to the limitations of human fortune, it also denies them. Because Odysseus' poverty and even his old age are represented as parts of a disguise, they are not inescapable conditions imposed on him by fortune but temporary and inessential states that he can shed at will. His apparent decline does not represent susceptibility to the changes that come with time, but rather a deliberately manipulated falsehood. Odysseus' disguise testifies to the reality of the suitors' challenge, but also belittles it; it is a sign of their temporary ascendance, but also a resource that assures his eventual and inevitable triumph over them. Thus the weakness to which Odysseus' disguise testifies is cast in an ironic light; its significance is always tempered by the audience's awareness of the reality that will be revealed when Odysseus' true identity becomes known.

Odysseus' disguise allows him to turn the humiliation imposed on him by his enemies into a defense against them. More broadly, the idea it dramatizes—that seeming debilities can be seen as part of a deliberately assumed disguise—offers a defense against the painful experience of powerlessness. The representation of weakness as a disguise implies that people are not themselves unless they are at their most impressive. In the specific context of the Homeric epics, the strategy of disguise overcomes the problem experienced by Achilles and other heroes in the *Iliad*, the problem of how a hero can survive a situation in which the honor through which he is identified to himself and to the world is not steadily available to him.[10] This victory shows why the conflict embedded in the epic tradition[11] between reliance on *bie*, "force," represented by Achilles, and reliance on *metis*, "guile," represented by Odysseus, is resolved in the *Odyssey* in favor of *mêtis*. The capacity for thinking one thing and saying another that goes with *mêtis*, allows the hero to tolerate and even to manipulate disjunctions between his own ongoing sense of merit and outer appearances. For a hero like Odysseus, who is characterized by the epithet "τολύτροπος," which includes among its connotations "versatility" and "adaptability," such disjunctions are not misfortunes but part of a plot that reflects Odysseus' ability to control not only himself but his fortunes. [12]

Notes

6. See Hermann Fränkel, *Early Greek Poetry and Philosophy*, 75–85; Alasdair MacIntyre, *After Virtue*, 114–122; James M. Redfield, *Nature and Culture in the* Iliad, 20–23.

7. E.g., *Il.* 8.161–166, where Hector, having put Diomedes to flight, taunts him by reminding him that the Achaeans used to honor him with the first place at feasts and predicting that they will no longer do so.

8. E.g., *Il.* 4.338–348, where Agamemnon accuses Odysseus and Mnestheus of enjoying the privileges of heroic status without really earning them.

9. For a thorough discussion and critique of attempts to explain Odysseus' seemingly illogical suppression of his name in Phaecia, see Bernard Fenik, *Studies in the Odyssey*, 7–18. Fenik's own view (which is in part a development of the discussion of irony and disguise in the *Odyssey* by Uvo Hölscher, *Untersuchungen zur Form der Odyssee*, 58–72) is that the poet is less interested in giving Odysseus a logically satisfactory motive than in developing the rich and characteristically Odyssean irony that pervades the episode as a result of Odysseus' secrecy. I would simply add that part of what that irony is about is the gap between Odysseus' actual reputation and the anonymous status he has among the Phaeacians. For the view that Odysseus does not give his name when Arete asks him to because he is not at that time fully himself, see Wilhelm Mattes, *Odysseus bei den Phäaken*, 133.

10. Thus, while Bruno Snell's claim that "In Homer, a ... separation between external and internal values is never made" (*The Discovery of the Mind*, 49) is certainly overstated, the *Odyssey*'s stress on disguise does not, as Joseph Russo has argued ("The Inner Man in Archilochus and the *Odyssey*," 145–146), exemplify a distinction between inner and outer values so much as an attempt to cope with fluctuations of external circumstances in the absence of such a distinction.

11. For a recent discussion of this conflict, see Gregory Nagy, *The Best of the Achaeans*, 45–49.

12. On *mêtis* as a quality that protects against the vicissitudes of time, see Marcel Detienne and Jean-Pierre Vernant, *Cunning Intelligence in Greek Culture and Society*, esp. 13–14, 20. As Detienne and Vernant point out, the nature of the man who is *polutropos* can be apprehended in the way he resembles the man who is *ephêmeros*, who represents the extreme of susceptibility to fortune and change, but with the crucial difference that the one who is *polutropos* actively controls his mutability. "The *polutropos* one, on the other hand, is distinguished by the control he possesses: subtle and shifting as he is, he is always master of himself and is only unstable in appearance" (40).

Works by Homer

In Greek:

Opera. Ed Demetrios Chalkokondyles, 1488.

Odysseia. Ed. Aldo Pio Manuzio, 1504.

Ilias et Odyssea. Ed. J. Micyllus, 1541.

Works. Eds. Jacobus Micyllus and Joachim Camerarius, 1541.

Ilias. Ed. Ioannis Crespini Atrebatii, 1559.

Ilias. Ed. Johann Guenther, 1563.

Ilias. Ed. Georgius Bishop, 1591.

Opera. Ed. Johannes Field, 1660.

Ilias. Ed. Johnanes Hayes, 1679.

Ilias. Ed. Thomas Day Seymour, 1695.

Opera. Ed. Samuel Clarke, 1740.

Works. Eds. Thomas Grenville, Richard Porson, et al., 1800.

Ilias et Odyssea. Ed. Richard Payne Knight, 1820.

Works. Ed. Wilhelm Dindorf, 1828.

Odyssey. Ed. Henry Hayman, 1882.

Odyssea. Ed. Arthur Ludwich, 1890.

Ilias. Ed. Dominicus Comparetti, 1901.

Opera. Eds. David B. Monro and Thomas W. Allen, 1912.

Odyssey. Ed. A. T. Murray, 1919.

Ilias et Odyssea. Ed. Eduardi Schwartz, 1924.

Odyssey. Ed. W. B. Stanford, 1948.

Odyssea. Ed. Helmut van Thiel, 1991.

Translated into English

The Whole Works of Homer. Trans. George Chapman, 1612.

Odyssey. Trans. John Ogilby, 1659.

Iliad. Trans. John Ogilby, 1660.

The Iliad and Odyssey of Homer. Trans. Thomas Hobbes, 1673.

The Iliad of Homer. Trans. Alexander Pope, 1720.

The Odyssey of Homer. Trans. Alexander Pope, William Broome, and Elijah Fenton, 1726.

The Iliad of Homer. Trans. James Macpherson, 1773.

The Iliad and Odyssey of Homer. Trans. William Cowper, 1791.

The Iliad of Homer. Trans. William Cullen Bryant, 1870.

The Odyssey of Homer. Trans. William Cullen Bryant, 1872.

The Odyssey of Homer. Trans. S. H. Butcher and Andrew Lang, 1879.

Iliad. Trans. Andrew Lang, Walter Leaf, and Ernest Myers, 1883.

The Odyssey of Homer. Trans. Willliam Morris, 1887.

The Odyssey of Homer. Trans. George Herbert Palmer, 1891.

The Iliad of Homer. Trans. Samuel Butler, 1898.

The Odyssey of Homer. Trans. Samuel Butler, 1900.

Iliad. Trans. A. T. Murray, 1924.

Odyssey. Trans. A. T. Murray, 1931.

The Odyssey of Homer. Trans. T. E. Lawrence, 1932.

Iliad. Trans. W. H. D. Rouse, 1937.

The Story of Odysseus. Trans. W. H. D. Rouse, 1942.

Iliad. Trans. Richmond Lattimore, 1951.

Odyssey. Trans. Robert Fitzgerald, 1961.

Odyssey. Trans. Richmond Lattimore, 1967.

Iliad. Trans. Robert Fitzgerald, 1974.

The *Iliad*. Trans. Martin Hammond, 1987.

The *Iliad*. Trans. Robert Fagles, 1990.

The *Iliad*. Trans. Ennis Rees, 1991.

The *Iliad*. Trans. Michael Pierce Reck, 1994.

The *Iliad*. Trans. Stanley Lombardo, 1997.

The *Iliad*. Trans. A. T. Murray (revised by William F. Wyatt), 1999.

 Annotated Bibliography

Auerbach, Erich. 1957. "Odysseus' Scar." In *Mimesis: The Representation of Reality in Western Literature*. Trans. Willard Trask. New York.

Auerbach's basic procedure in this broad history of Western literary representation is to quote a lengthy passage from a major text and to discuss its stylistic and intellectual features, and to speculate brilliantly, if exaggeratedly, on its conception of "reality." The first chapter is on Homer. He quotes the recognition scene between Odysseus and Eurycleia, and argues that Homeric narrative is entirely externalized, in an absolute present. He juxtaposes Homer's recognition scene to the binding of Isaac from the Old Testament, which is a more inward and elliptical mode of narrative.

Austin, Norman. 1972. *Archery at the Dark of the Moon: Poetic Problems in Homer's "Odyssey."* Berkeley and Los Angeles.

Austin's stated purpose is to free Homer of "the condescension prevalent in Homeric scholarship" and so sensitize critics to Homer's "depth." He traces this "condescension" to two sources: the primitivism implicit in Milman Parry's and Bruno Snell's work. The first chapter questions Parry's oral-formulaic paradigm by showing that Odysseus' most common epithets are statistically infrequent, and that they occur only in specific, localized contexts. His final two chapters discuss literary and interpretive issues: first, the re-establishment of *homophrosyne* with his wife and other members of his house; and second, more controversially, the cosmic underpinnings of Odysseus' return, which seem to align with the coming of spring.

Clarke, W. 1981. *Homer's Readers: A Historical Introduction to the* Iliad *and the* Odyssey. East Brunswick.

This is not a book on historical background, but a history of the reception, criticism, and appreciation of the Homeric poems. Especially helpful are the final two chapters, "Homer Analyzed" and "Homer Anatomized." The first is a sober account of the Homeric Question since Wolf's *Prolegomena*, the second charts the current position of Homeric scholarship.

Clay, J. 1983. *The Wrath of Athena: Gods and Men in the* Odyssey. Princeton.

The central argument of this book is that Athena's anger towards Odysseus is decisive in shaping happenings of the *Odyssey*. Book I marks the resolution of Athena's wrath and so the beginning of Odysseus' homeward movements. This argument is embedded in more general reflections on the relationship of the divine and human in the *Odyssey*.

Cohen, B., ed. 1995. *The Distaff Side: Representing the Female in* Homer's Odyssey. New York and Oxford.

The eleven essays contained in this volume are divided into three sections: Introduction, Female Representations in the *Odyssey*, and Representations of Female Characters for the *Odyssey* in Ancient Art. Especially incisive contributions come from Helene Foley, on Penelope as a moral agent; Sheila Murnaghan, on the implications of Athena's controlling role in the poem; and Froma Zeitlin, on Odysseus' bed as a symbol of Penelope's fidelity.

Detienne, M. and J.-P. Vernant. 1989. *Cunning Intelligence in Greek Culture and Society*. Trans. J. Lloyd. Sussex and

Atlantic Highlands, N.J. [First Publication 1974. *Les Ruses de l'intelligence: La Métis des Grecs*. Paris].

A structuralist analysis by two French critics of the role of *metis*—cunning or practical intelligence—in Greek society over several centuries. Odysseus is the first and most important practitioner of this form of intelligence.

Edwards, A. 1985. *Achilles in the* Odyssey: *Ideologies of Heroism in the Homeric Epic*, Königsten.

"This book is a study of the *Odyssey's* reception of Achilles as he is known from the *Iliad*" (1). Edwards argues that Achilles and Odysseus are two opposing ethical and poetic paradigms. He traces the portrayal of this opposition in the *Odyssey*.

Fenik, B. 1974. *Studies in the* Odyssey. *Hermes Einzelschriften*, no. 30. Wiesbaden.

The purpose of this book is to explain apparent anomalies and inconsistencies in the *Odyssey*—often taken by analyst critics as evidence for interpolation and multiple authorship—in terms of Homer's general narrative techniques and tendencies. The first section looks at the difficulties surrounding Odysseus' meeting with Arete in Book VII, and the second section looks at "doublets:" characters or incidents that bear striking similarities to other characters or incidents in the poem.

Finley, M.I. 1954. *The World of Odysseus*. New York. [Revised edition, 1978. New York and London.]

Finley's book remains the best introduction to the historical and sociological background of the Homeric poems.

Foley, H. P. 1978. "'Reverse Similes' and Sex Roles in the *Odyssey*." *Arethusa* 11:7–26.

Foley calls a simile in which the subject changes gender a "reverse similes." In this important study she discusses these similes as symptoms of the *Odyssey*'s comedic structure of social disruption and restoration, and argues that they reveal the interdependence of Odysseus and Penelope in the return plot.

Goldhill, S. 1991. *The Poet's Voice: Essays on Poetics and Greek Literature*. Cambridge.

"The project of this book is to investigate how poetry and the figure of the poet are represented, discussed, contested within the poetry of ancient Greece" (ix). Goldhill defines the poet's voice by three interrelated concepts: representation, intertextuality, and self-reflexiveness. His first chapter discusses the parallels of Odysseus and Homer as tellers of tales, and the *Odyssey*'s explorations of man as a user of language.

Graziosi, B., and J. Haubold. 2005. *Homer: The Resonance of Epic*. London.

A highly accessible and clearly written investigation of the implications of the various scholarly discoveries of the twentieth century, and how they should affect our appreciation and interpretation of the poems. Graziosi and Haubold explain the traditional elements of epic diction and style in terms of "resonance"—that is, their ability to evoke a much larger web of myth and cosmic history.

Morris, I., and Powell, B., eds. 1996. *A New Companion to Homer*. Leiden, N.Y., and Koln.

This volume is a comprehensive collection of essays that will introduce readers to modern Homeric scholarship. The book is organized into four sections: first, Transmission and History of Interpretation; second, Homer's Language; third, Homer as Literature; fourth, Homer's Worlds.

Murnaghan, Sheila. 1987. *Disguise and Recognition in the* Odyssey. Princeton.

Murnaghan's study has become the standard treatment of this important theme. She discusses Odysseus' capacity for disguise as his distinguishing feature, and characteristic of his peculiar mode of heroism. Also helpful and sensitive is her treatment of Penelope (Chap. 4).

Nagy, Gregory. 1979. *The Best of the Achaeans: Concepts of the Hero in Archaic Greek Poetry*. Baltimore and London.

This book is primarily concerned with the figure of Achilles, but has helpful sections on Odysseus. Nagy links Homeric poetry to pre-Greek, Indo-European archetypes, and he attributes Achilles' preeminence as a hero among the Greeks to his close association with elemental forces of nature, which makes him an heir of an old Indo-European tradition. Nagy draws important comparisons between Achilles and Odysseus as exemplars of *bie* (force) and *metis* (intelligence), and *kleos* and *nostos*, respectively.

Parry, M. 1971. *The Making of Homeric Verse: The Collected Essays of Milman Parry*. Ed. A. Parry. Oxford.

Milman Parry was the first to comprehensively link the Homeric formula to a long tradition of oral poetry, and his work has had a profound and lingering impact on Homeric studies. Any student interested in oral theory or the traditional element of the Homeric poems should begin with Parry.

Pucci, P. 1987. *Odysseus Polutropos: Intertextual in the* Odyssey *and* Iliad. Ithaca, N.Y., and London.

As the subtitle suggests, Pucci offers a series of "intertextual" readings; that is, he exposes how the epics allude to each other, often agonistically. His premise is that the *Iliad* and *Odyssey* developed within a milieu or tradition which the epics participate in and comment on. He borrows much from modern theoretical criticism, including Derrida and Barthes. Particularly illuminating, I think, is Part III, which investigates the troubling synonymy of *thumos* and *gaster* in the *Odyssey*.

Schein, S, ed. 1996. *Reading the* Odyssey: *Selected Interpretive Essays*. Princeton.

An excellent modern selection of essays on the *Odyssey*, including selections from French, German, and Anglo-American classicists. Rather than being a generalized study, these essays cluster around a set of focuses: gender roles and the character of Penelope, the representation of social and religious institutions, and defining Odysseus' brand of heroism.

Segal, C. 1994. *Singers, Heroes, and Gods in the* Odyssey. Ithaca, N.Y.

A collection of 10 essays by one of America's most prominent classicists. The book is composed of three discreet sections unified by consistency of approach: the first section discusses the mythical and psychological underpinnings of Odysseus' voyages; the second investigates the figure of the poet and the neglected books between Odysseus' landing on Ithaca and his arrival at the palace; and the third the role of the gods. Especially famous and insightful is Chapter 5, "*Kleos* and its Ironies."

Vidal-Naquet, P. 1981. "Land and Sacrifice in the *Odyssey*: A Study of Religious and Mythical Meanings." In *Myth, Religion and Society: Structuralist Essays by M. Detienne, L. Gernet, J.-P. Vernant, and P. Vidal-Naquet*. Ed. R.L. Gordon. Cambridge-Paris. [First publication 1970. "Valeurs religieuses et mythiques de la terre et du sacrifice dans l'*Odyssée*." *Annales E.S.C.* 25: 1278–1297.]

Beginning with an analysis of Hesiod's myth of the golden age, Vidal-Naquet looks at the presentation of land, agriculture, and sacrifice in the *Odyssey* as they relate to social organization and frame Odysseus' return to humanity.

Contributors

Harold Bloom is Sterling Professor of the Humanities at Yale University. He is the author of 30 books, including *Shelley's Mythmaking* (1959), *The Visionary Company* (1961), *Blake's Apocalypse* (1963), *Yeats* (1970), *A Map of Misreading* (1975), *Kabbalah and Criticism* (1975), *Agon: Toward a Theory of Revisionism* (1982), *The American Religion* (1992), *The Western Canon* (1994), and *Omens of Millennium: The Gnosis of Angels, Dreams, and Resurrection* (1996). *The Anxiety of Influence* (1973) sets forth Professor Bloom's provocative theory of the literary relationships between the great writers and their predecessors. His most recent books include *Shakespeare: The Invention of the Human* (1998), a 1998 National Book Award finalist, *How to Read and Why* (2000), *Genius: A Mosaic of One Hundred Exemplary Creative Minds* (2002), *Hamlet: Poem Unlimited* (2003), *Where Shall Wisdom Be Found?* (2004), and *Jesus and Yahweh: The Names Divine* (2005). In 1999, Professor Bloom received the prestigious American Academy of Arts and Letters Gold Medal for Criticism. He has also received the International Prize of Catalonia, the Alfonso Reyes Prize of Mexico, and the Hans Christian Andersen Bicentennial Prize of Denmark.

Thomas P. Schmidt received his BA in Classics from Yale University, where he received the Curtis Prize for literary criticism and the Winthrop Prize for excellence in Greek. He is currently the Mellon Fellow at Clare College, Cambridge.

Longinus was a Greek teacher of rhetoric who lived in Athens. The classic work of criticism, *On the Sublime*, was long attributed to Longinus, but is now attributed to the author named Pseudo-Longinus, who lived in the first century A.D.

Erich Auerbach taught at the University of Marburg, Pennsylvania State University, Princeton University, and finally as Sterling Professor of Romance Philology at Yale University. His works include *Dante: Poet of the Secular World* (1961), *Mimesis: The Representation of Reality in Western Literature* (1953), and *Literary Language and its Public in Late Latin Antiquity and in the Middle Ages* (1965).

Milman Parry was an associate professor of Greek at Harvard University. His collected papers were published posthumously in *The Making of Homeric Verse: The Collected Papers of Milman Parry* (1971).

Simon Goldhill is professor of Greek Literature and Culture at Cambridge University. His works include *Language, Sexuality, Narrative: The* Oresteia (1984), *Reading Greek Tragedy* (1986), *The Poet's Voice* (1991), and *Foucault's Virginity* (1995).

Pierre Vidal-Naquet is Director and co-founder of the Centre Louis Gernet at the École des Hautes Études en Sciences Sociales in Paris. His works include *Le Chasseur noir: Formes de pensée et forms de société dans le monde grec* and *Mythe et tragédie en Grèce ancienne* (with Jean-Pierre Vernant).

Jean-Pierre Vernant is professor emeritus of the Collège de France, where he held the Chair of Comparative Studies in Ancient Religions. His works include *Les Origines de la pensée grecque*, *Mythe et pensée chez les grecs*, *Mythe et société en Grèce ancienne*, *Mythe et tragédie en Grèce ancienne* (with Pierre Vidal-Naquet), and *Les Ruses de l'intelligence: La Métis des Grecs* (with Marcel Detienne).

Jean Starobinski is professor emeritus of French Literature at the University of Geneva. His works include *Words Upon Words: The Anagram of Ferdinand De Saussure* (1979), *1789: The Emblems of Reason* (1982), *Montaigne in Motion* (1985), *The Invention of Liberty: 1700–1789* (1987), *La Melancholie Au Miroir: Trois Lectures De Baudelaire* (1989), *Blessings in Disguise, or, the Morality of Evil* (1993), and *Largesse* (1994).

Froma I. Zeitlin's works include *Under the Sign of the Shield: Semiotics and Aeschylus'* Seven Against Thebes (1982), *Playing the Other: Gender and Society in Classical Greek Culture* (1996), "Staging Dionysus Between Thebes and Athens" (1993), and "Figuring Fidelity in Homer's *Odyssey*" (1995).

Charles Segal was the Walter C. Kleit professor of the Classics at Harvard University. His works include *The Theme of the Mutilation of the Corpse in the* Iliad (1971), *Tragedy and Civilization: An Interpretation of Sophocles* (1981), *Poetry and Myth in Ancient Pastoral: Essays on Theocritus and Virgil* (1981), *Pindar's Mythmaking: The Fourth Pythian Ode* (1986), *Orpheus: The Myth of the Poet* (1986), and *Singers, Heroes, and Gods in the* Odyssey (1994).

Helene P. Foley is professor of Classics at Barnard College. Her works include *Reflections of Women in Antiquity* (ed. 1981), *Ritual Irony: Poetry and Sacrifice in Euripides* (1985), and *The Homeric Hymn to Demeter: Translation, Commentary, and Interpretive Essays* (ed. 1994).

Sheila Murnaghan is the Alfred Reginald Allen Memorial Professor of Greek at the University of Pennsylvania. Her works include *Disguise and Recognition in the* Odyssey (1987), and *Women and Slaves in Greco-Roman Culture: Differential Equations* (co-edited with Sandra Joshel, 1998).

Acknowledgments

Longinus, "On the Sublime," translated by W.H. Fyfe, pp. 191–197. © 1995 by the President and Fellows of Harvard University Press. Reprinted by permission of President and Fellows of Harvard University Press.

Auerbach, Eric, *Mimesis*, pp. 5–7, 13–14. © 1953 Princeton University Press, 1981 renewed Princeton University Press, 2003 paperback edition. Reprinted by permission of Princeton University Pres.

The Making of Homeric Verse: The Collected Papers of Milman Parry, edited by Adam Parry, pp. 9, 13–14, 21–22. © 1971 by Clarendon Press. By permission of Oxford University Press, Inc.

Simon Goldhill, *The Poet's Voice: Essays on Poetics and Greek Literature*, pp. 1–5. © 1991 by Cambridge University Press. Reprinted with the permission of Cambridge University Press.

Pierre Vidal-Naquet, "Land and Sacrifice in the Odyssey: A Study of Religious and Mythical Meanings", edited by R.L. Gordon, pp. 83–85. © 1981 by Cambridge University Press. Reprinted with the permission of Cambridge University Press.

Schein, Seth L., *Reading the Odyssey*, pp. 187–189. © 1996 Princeton University Press. Reprinted by permission of Princeton University Press.

Starobinski, Jean, "The Inside and the Outside." *The Hudson Review* 25, no. 28 (Autumn 1975), pp. 345–347, 348–351. © 1975 *The Hudson Review*. Reprinted by permission.

Index

Characters in literary works are indexed by first name (if any), followed by the name of the work in parentheses